THE CURTISS HS FLYING BOATS

THE CURTISS HS FLYING BOATS

K.M. Molson

A.J. Shortt

NAVAL INSTITUTE PRESS

ANNAPOLIS, MARYLAND

First published in the United States of America by the Naval Institute Press, 118 Maryland Avenue, Annapolis, Maryland 21402-5035.

Library of Congress Catalog Card Number 94-74868
ISBN 1-55750-142-4
Cataloging in Publication Data is available from the Library of Congress

Editorial Note:
In Parts I and II all measurements, where appropriate, are given in metric followed by the imperial equivalents in parentheses. Aircraft specifications in Part III are given first in the original manufacturer's measurements and followed by the metric equivalents in parentheses.

Sources for all illustrative material are credited, in parentheses, at the end of the corresponding captions. Every effort has been made to obtain permission from copyright holders to reprint this material. In some cases, copyright holders could not be found. Errors and omissions will be corrected in future editions.

Excerpt from *Under My Wings,* by Basil L. Rowe, included in Chapter 5 is reprinted with the permission of Macmillan Publishing Company. Copyright 1956 by Basil L. Rowe, renewed 1984 by Carl Rowe and Mrs. Lewis White.

Printed in Canada on acid-free paper

TABLE OF CONTENTS

FOREWORD

The Curtiss HS-2L flying boat played a unique role in the development of aviation in Canada. Among its many accomplishments, the HS-2L inaugurated the bush-flying tradition indelibly linked to Canada for over seventy years. The type also pioneered many of the ways in which a new technology could be used to develop a young and dynamic country. We are all beneficiaries of this legacy.

K.M. Molson and A.J. Shortt tell the tale of this unprepossessing but critically important type and the construction of the National Aviation Museum's example in the first volume of *Profiles in Aeronautical History*, a monographic series about the aircraft in the Museum's collection. Molson and Shortt fill a gap in our knowledge about the history of the type and its use in Canada and elsewhere. They also document for posterity the dedication, skill and resourcefulness of the Museum team that reproduced the only example of the HS-2L now in existence. Future monographs will cover the history and restoration of other important aircraft in the Museum's collection.

The National Aviation Museum's reproduction of a Curtiss HS-2L acknowledges the type's significance in Canada's aviation heritage. This volume is conclusive testimony to that fact.

C.J. Terry
Director-General
National Aviation Museum

ACKNOWLEDGEMENTS

A historical book invariably needs the assistance of many who have knowledge of the subject and related matters and this is particularly true when a number of different countries are involved. Accordingly, I am most grateful to the many who have assisted me in the preparation of this book. Their names are listed below.

Dan-San Abbott; Richard S. Allen; C. Gordon Ballentine; John Barton, NAM; Peter M. Bowers; Hugo T. Byettebier; Louis S. Casey; Robert L. Cavanaugh; Dr Kenneth A. Cheesman; Mrs. Edward J. Cooper; Peter Corley-Smith, RBCM; D.Dufriche; W.E. (Tony) Doherty, GHCM; Lindsley A. Dunn, GHCM; John M. Elliott; Harry Gann; Robert A. Gordon; Bartlett Gould; John A. Griffin; Daniel P. Hagedorn, NASM; Fransisco Halbritter; Gordon R. Hutt; Jack F. Hyde; Roger W. Ingalls; John L. Johnson Jr.; Terry Judge; Walter (Bill) Kahre; Harvey Lippincott, NEAM; R. Liebermann; Bradbury McLelland; Robert C. Mikesh; Robert B. Meyers Jr.; W. Ross Richardson; B. Risseeu; A.J. (Fred) Shortt, NAM; Dr Paul G. Spitzer, Boeing Co.; Robert W. Stevens; James Thompson; Patrick J. Tully; John W. Underwood; I. (Pete) Vachon; Jay Veith; Pierre Verhelst, OBH; Ray Wagner, SDAM; Charles G. Worman, USAFM.

While the main contributors to this book are noted above, other NAM staff members have assisted me from time to time, and to them also I am grateful.

I must make special mention of John (Jack) M. Elliott, a long-time friend, retired Major of the U.S. Marine Corps and historian with the U.S. Navy. Jack's help has been invaluable in many ways to the production of this book.

Finally, I owe considerable thanks to my wife, Frances, who has helped in many ways and once again tolerated the inconvenience of me working on another book.

K.M. Molson

I would like to thank the following people for their assistance: C.J. Terry, Dorothy Fields, Claudette St-Hilaire, R.W. Bradford, J. Dorn, B.D. Mackeracher, H.P. Jessen, J. Barton, and K.M. Molson.

A.J. Shortt

PART I

CURTISS HS FLYING BOATS

K.M. Molson

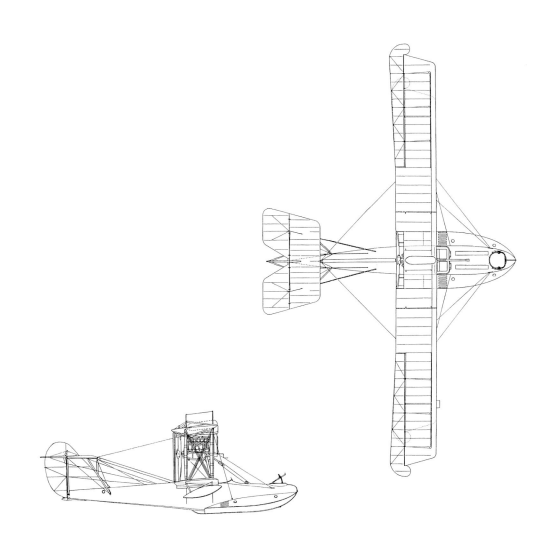

Chapter 1

GLENN HAMMOND CURTISS AND WATER-BASED AIRCRAFT

The world's first powered flight took place on December 17, 1903, when the Wright brothers flew their landplane. It was not until over six years later, on March 28, 1910, that the first water-based aircraft took off, and Henri Fabre made the first seaplane flight near Marseilles, France, in his odd tandem-wing monoplane. However, the seaplane proved to be stillborn. Neither the Fabre airframe nor its floatation gear proved capable of further development. The seaplane had to wait until January 1911 for its practical beginning when Glenn Hammond Curtiss made a successful public flight at San Diego, California, on a Curtiss D pusher mounted on a single central float, which he called his "hydro-aeroplane" or simply his "hydro."

Glenn Hammond Curtiss was a native of Hammondsport, New York, and began his career first by selling bicycles, then by making them, and then by making motorcycles and their engines. His reputation for making good engines led to an invitation to join the Aerial Experiment Association (AEA) being formed at Baddeck, Nova Scotia, by Dr Alexander Graham Bell. Curtiss was appointed Director of Experiments and assigned Project Engineer to the AEA's

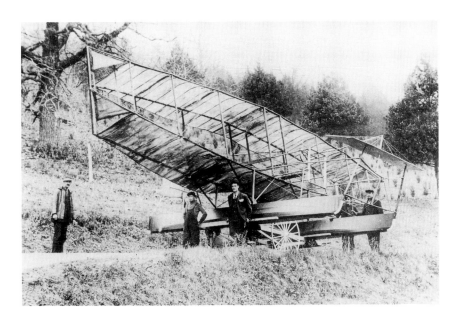

Curtiss, standing at far left, first attempted to fly a water-based aircraft with J.A.D. McCurdy when the AEA June Bug *was fitted with floats and the Silver Dart's more powerful engine. Unsuccessful attempts were made in 1907 and 1909. (GHCM)*

third aircraft, the *June Bug*. It was awarded the *Scientific American* Trophy for making the first public flight in America in July 1908. Curtiss went on to show his interest in water-based aircraft by making a pair of canoe-like floats to mount on the *June Bug*. The aircraft was then renamed the *Loon* and tested on Lake Keuka at Hammondsport in November 1908. It was unsuccessful, even when fitted with the more powerful engine of the AEA's fourth aircraft, the *Silver Dart*.

A production model of the Curtiss E HYDRO with Curtiss at the controls. The first practical seaplane was the similar, but shorter-span HYDRO D. (GHCM)

The world's first successful flying boat, the prototype Curtiss E, flew with Curtiss at the controls in July, 1912 on Lake Keuka, Hammondsport, N.Y. It was flown with and without wing extensions and the forward elevator was later removed. (GHCM)

After the success of the *Silver Dart* the AEA disbanded and its American patents were assigned to Curtiss. Curtiss started his own company and designed a series of successful pusher biplanes derived from the AEA machines, which also had the unusual feature of being quickly dismantled and packed in 1.8-m (6-ft) long boxes for easy transport. These biplanes proved successful and were sold to individuals and the U.S. Signal Corps. Curtiss then installed a single float on a Curtiss Model D pusher, and after unsuccessful early trials flew it successfully, as noted, in 1911. On February 25, 1911, an amphibious version called the *Triad* was successfully flown. The Model E pusher was successfully flown on a single float in June 1911, and examples were sold to the U.S. Navy (USN) and others over the next two or three years – the first really practical seaplanes.

This success was followed by the introduction of the flying boat, whose conception and successful creation were entirely due to Curtiss. He envisaged a flying machine whose boat-like floatation gear also housed the crew and passengers so that it became a true flying boat. After the first inevitable failures, his first successful

A Curtiss F flying boat of the Curtiss Aviation School, Toronto. The success of the Curtiss E and F models established Curtiss throughout the aviation world as the name in water-based aircraft. They were used in many countries and the USN used the F boat for training as late as 1918. (E.R. Grange)

flying boat became airborne in July 1912. It was developed shortly thereafter in the E and F models that would be used widely by both civil and military clients both in North America and abroad.

In 1914 the twin-engined Curtiss H-1 *America* flying boat was built for a proposed transatlantic flight. This was the first large flying boat. After the proposed flight was called off at the outbreak of World War I, the flying boat was sold to the Royal Naval Air Service (RNAS), predecessor of a long line of Model H flying boats that benefited greatly from improved hull designs contributed by Commander John Porte, RNAS. In 1915 Curtiss developed the Model K, his first high-powered single-engine flying boat. Although 53 Model Ks were made and the airframe apparently was satisfactory, power plant problems caused difficulties and the type was not considered successful.

A Curtiss hydro-aeroplane reproduction flown in June 1986 at Hammondsport, N.Y., to celebrate the 75th anniversary of the USN's first aircraft acquisition. (K.M. Molson)

Curtiss not only developed the first practical seaplanes in both floatplane and flying boat forms but went on to develop the first large twin-engine flying boats. These innovations may be considered Curtiss's foremost contribution to aviation.

Chapter 2

THE CURTISS HS

FLYING BOATS:

DEVELOPMENT AND

PRODUCTION

The Curtiss HS-1

In the early spring of 1917 Curtiss again undertook the design of a high-powered single-engine flying boat. To expedite design and construction he used the hull of the H-14, a twin-engine flying boat that had been designed for the U.S. Army and proved unsuccessful. The new machine was designated the HS-1, signifying "Model H, single-engine, first version." The hull seated a crew of two side-by-side in a cockpit just forward of the lower wing, with no provision for armament or payload. The engine, a Curtiss V2 of 200 hp, was installed as a pusher driving a three-blade wood propeller. The hull was of planked-wood construction while the wing and tail surfaces were of conventional wood construction with the exception of the steel-tube rudder.

The sole two-place Curtiss H-14, whose hull was adopted for the HS-1, on Lake Keuka in 1917. It had two pusher 100 hp Curtiss OXX engines, an upper wingspan of 17-m (55-ft 9 $\frac{1}{8}$ -in.) length and 11.7-m (38-ft 5 $\frac{5}{8}$ -in.) width, a gross wt. of 1950 kg (4,290 lb.) and a maximum speed of 105 km/h (65 mph). (GHCM)

The HS-1 on July 18, 1917. (GHCM)

The HS-1 prototype was first flown from the Niagara River at Buffalo, New York, about the end of June. Its pilot, Harold D. Kantner, flew it for most, if not all, of its early test flights. Kantner had learned to fly at the Moisant Flying School at Mineola, Long Island, New York, in the spring of 1911. He remained active in aviation as a pilot and designer until retiring about 1970. On July 23 he flew the HS-1 from Buffalo to Detroit, Michigan, with a passenger,

HS-1 at Buffalo on July 18, 1917. A USN officer is in the right-hand seat of the aircraft. (GHCM)

and made one stop at Toledo, Ohio – a distance of about 435 km (270 mi.). They returned the next day and the flight received considerable publicity. During the early test flying a USN observer was on hand.

A number of significant events after the start of the HS-1 project greatly affected the type and its development. First, the United States declared war on Germany on April 6. Then, the USN decided that it would have to provide aerial protection for ships carrying troops to France and that German submarines could soon be expected to harass shipping on the east coast of North America. Further, it was thought that since the patrol aircraft would be operating beyond the range of German machines, defensive armament would not be required on the aircraft. A high-powered single-engine flying boat carrying depth charges and a single forward-mounted machine gun would be adequate rather than the larger twin-engine aircraft required for patrols flown from Britain.

Also at that time, the United States had military aircraft suitable only for training so the "Bolling Mission" went to Europe in mid-June to see what types of aircraft the Allies might have that would be suitable for adoption by the United States. Of course, a high-powered single-engine flying boat was on the shopping list; however, when the Mission reported back two months later, it noted that no such machine was available in Europe.

Meanwhile, in the United States, soon after the declaration of war, it was decided to standardize an engine design that could be made in three versions: a 4-cylinder version of 100 hp for trainers; a 6-cylinder version of 150 hp for fighters; and a 12-cylinder version to be made in two models, a low-compression one of 360 hp for the USN and a high-compression one of 400 hp for the United States Air Service (USAS). The Hall-Scott Motor Car Co. and the Packard Motor Car Co. both had a promising 12-cylinder engine under testing. The chief engineers of both companies were brought together and they quickly combined the best features of each of their engines to yield a new engine, called the Liberty. The fact that tools for most parts were available in both companies was responsible for the remarkable speed in getting the Liberty into production. The first Liberty, an 8-cylinder version, was flown in a Lowe, Willard & Fowler (LWF) Model F that was especially modified from the LWF Model V2 to suit the Liberty. It made its first flight at Buffalo, New York, on August 29, 1917.

The USN conducted the first ground test of the 12-cylinder Liberty engine and then it was installed in the HS-1. However, Chief Instructor David H. McCulloch of the Curtiss School first flew the HS-1 on October 10, 1917, with a Curtiss VX3 installed, and an improved version of the original V2; test figures were recorded. A 360-hp 12-cylinder Liberty, the third one built, was then installed and the HS-1 was flown again by McCulloch on October 21 – the first 12-cylinder Liberty-powered flight. Roland Rohlfs, Curtiss Experimental Pilot, then took over and made two flights on October 22.

Curtiss HS-1L and HS-2L

The USN was satisfied with the test results of both engine and airframe and accepted the Liberty-powered HS-1 with suitable modifications for naval use – which in this form became the HS-1L. A bow cockpit, complete with a Scarff ring-mounting for a Lewis gun, had to be installed; two racks to carry an 82-kg (180-lb) depth charge each (or an equivalent bomb load) also had to be installed, one under each wing. To bear the additional load the wing had to be enlarged by an additional 2.5 m² (27 sq. ft). In addition, a new fuel system was

Pioneer American pilot Harold D. Kantner in the HS-1. The HS-1 cockpit was generous and round in comparison to the oval cockpit of the HS-1L and HS-2L. (J.W. Underwood)

The three-dimensional serial number plate mounted on Curtiss flying boats was, and remains, unique. Similar plates are normally just flat metal. The plate shown here in full size is installed in the NAM specimen, but is not from any of the three aircraft used in the reconstruction. (K.M. Molson)

introduced. While not readily noticeable, it had some interesting features. Three fuel tanks were installed in the mid-portion of the hull, and a cylindrical gravity tank was installed above the upper-wing centre section. Each hull tank had its own fuel gauge, which projected above the hull and was visible to the crew. When starting and

Short wings with only three bays and the cylindrical gravity tank on the upper wing distinguish the HS-1L from the larger HS-2L. On the upper wing is a wind-driven generator for an experimental radio installation. (Source unknown)

until airborne, the crew hand-pumped fuel with a cockpit pump to the gravity tank. Then a wind-driven fan took over the pumping. A sight gauge was provided to enable the crew to verify that fuel was being pumped to the gravity tank. Interestingly enough, the HS-1L handbook shows a drawing of the machine with the HS-1 vertical tail. No photograph has been found of an HS-1L fitted with such a tail, but

Nose cockpit with Scarff ring-mounting for a Lewis gun. A bearing compass is mounted in front. (Boeing P197)

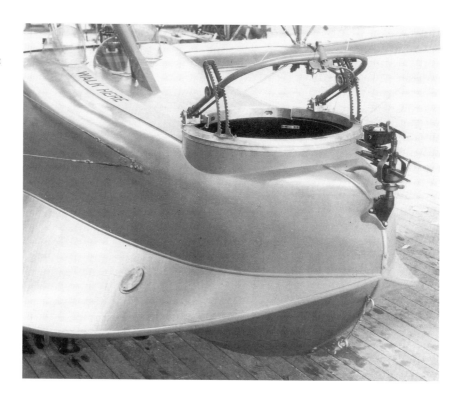

This view of the top-centre portion of the hull shows details of the interesting and unusual fuel system of the HS-1L/HS-2L. (K.M. Molson)

HS-2L with a Davis gun and a Lewis gun mounted as an aiming aid. (Peter M. Bowers)

it is possible the prototype was briefly flown with it and then the tail was later replaced.

As noted earlier, the Lewis gun was fitted to the HS-1L as its standard equipment. However, a number of machines, both HS-1Ls and HS-2Ls, were fitted with the Davis gun in place of the Lewis. This was an unusual weapon patented in 1911 by Commander Cleland Davis, USN, and it fired a projectile toward its target while simultaneously firing an equal weight of lead shot in the opposite direction. This arrangement neutralized normal recoil – beneficial to any lightweight weapons carrier like an aircraft. The air services of both Britain and the United States experimented with the Davis gun, and both countries conducted service trials. The USN selected the HS-1L and HS-2L to conduct service trials. Almost all patrol stations using the type had one or more machines fitted with 2.7-kg (6-lb) versions of the gun. Neither country adopted it for general use.

HS-1L A1599 at Buffalo on May 16, 1918, with wing extensions fitted to test their suitability for the proposed HS-2L. Almost invisible in the under-wing's shadow is a large bomb. Tests indicated the need for an enlarged rudder on the HS-2L. (GHCM.)

Curtiss shipped the HS-1L prototype, A800, promptly on January 4, 1918. Speed of delivery was possible because the HS-1L prototype was simply the modified HS-1. The next HS-1L was not shipped

The normal mounting of the Davis gun on an HS-1L or HS-2L. The under-wing bomb racks are under the lower wing. (USN)

A standard HS-2L showing its long wings, submerged gravity tank and enlarged rudder. It is leaving Anacostia NAS on a mail run to Hampton Roads NAS on January 7, 1919. Light snow is visible on the aircraft. (USNA)

until March 12. Meanwhile, the USN was anxious to equip its patrol stations quickly, so it issued contracts for the type to the LWF Engineering Co., College Point, Long Island, New York, and the Standard Aircraft Corp., Elizabeth, New Jersey. An oddity with the LWF contract is that 47 machines were noted at random on their record cards as being "cancelled," with no explanation. It is possible that they might have been accepted as spare components rather than as assembled aircraft. A listing of the cancelled serial numbers is noted elsewhere.

Production was just getting well under way when the USN received a message from Britain, saying that the 82-kg (180-lb) depth charge had been ineffective against submarines and strongly recommending a shift to the 104-kg (230-lb) depth charge. The USN looked into this and asked Curtiss if it would be possible to increase the wingspan by 3.7 m (12 ft) by fitting small panels in each side of the wing. The modification was agreed to. However, it was immediately found on trial that the HS-1L rudder was too small to suit the larger wing, and a rudder increased in area by 33 per cent was fitted. Also, a new centre section was installed; it partially enclosed the gravity tank and eliminated the earlier cylindrical gravity tank. These

Final assembly area for HS-2Ls in the Curtiss Buffalo plant. Curtiss was the largest maker of HS-1Ls and HS-2Ls and produced over half of the 1 218 machines built. (GHCM)

changes could be quickly made on the stations, and it was planned to convert all HS-1Ls to the new HS-2L standard by the end of the year. This wholesale conversion was not accomplished, partly because the

Assembling the hull of an HS-2L at the Boeing Air-plane Co., October 1918. (Boeing P121)

Final assembly area for HS-2Ls in the Gallaudet Aircraft Corp. plant in East Greenwich, Rhode Island. (CAHA)

Boeing-built HS-2Ls were unique because they had upper-wing ailerons only. (Boeing P192)

war ended with the Armistice in early November and partly because of inevitable delays. However, some machines were converted by stations almost immediately upon delivery.

More contracts were issued for the manufacture of HS-2Ls, including small contracts to two companies on the west coast, Loughead Aircraft Manufacturing Co., Santa Barbara, California, and the

Boeing Airplane Co., Seattle, Washington. This was the first U.S. government order received by Loughead (later Lockheed) and only the second received by Boeing. It is of interest that Boeing-built HS-2Ls differed from all others in having ailerons fitted to the upper wing only. The ailerons were reportedly slightly larger in chord than those on standard machines but dimensions are unknown. This simplification resulted from the Naval Aircraft Factory (NAF) experiments.

Two HS-2Ls were modified for special purposes by the NAF in Philadelphia, Pennsylvania, in the early postwar period, but no details of the changes or photographs of the machines have been found. The record card states that A2103 had folding wings fitted in 1919, was intended for use with the USN's first aircraft carrier, the USS *Langley*, then being fitted out (commissioned in early 1921). A2103 was tried out on the carrier, and its CO reported in an unpublished USN document of November 6, 1923: "The HS-2L flying boat allowed the *Langley* is thought to be undesirable for use on board, due to its great size, the difficulties in hoisting it in and out.... Therefore cancel the order for ones for the *Langley*."

Also, A1232 was fitted with a metal wing by the NAF in 1922. This wing was one of two designed and built by Charles Ward Hall, and was reported as being lighter than, but as serviceable as, the original. Hall was later President of the Hall Aluminum Aircraft Corp. of Buffalo.

It is of equal interest that in 1922 to 1923 the NAF fitted a number of surplus Curtiss R-6L twin-float seaplanes with HS wings. The resulting aircraft were designated NAF PT-1 and PT-2 Patrol Torpedo seaplanes. Some 15 PT-1s with HS-1L wings and 18 PT-2s with HS-2L wings were assembled.

The HS-1L and HS-2L were virtually the same airplane. Many HS-1Ls, but not all, were converted to HS-2L standards; if the two are considered as one basic type, it can be said that the total number produced, 1218, was the greatest for any flying boat made until then. This record stood after World War I until it was surpassed during World War II by the Consolidated PBY series of flying boats and amphibians with a total production in Canada, the United States, and the U.S.S.R. of over 3400. Because the demand for flying boats has diminished, it seems very likely that the PBY record figure will stand indefinitely.

During 1918, the Curtiss Engineering Corp., which had its plant at Garden City, Long Island, New York, and the NAF started a joint project to design and build a new flying boat designated the Curtiss HS-3 on its record cards but sometimes noted as the HS-3L elsewhere. It was an almost completely new type and should not be considered as an extension of the HS-1L/HS-2L design. However, brief mention is made here to round out the HS family story. The

Production of Curtiss HS-1L flying boats[1]

| Manufacturer | Serial Numbers | | Quantity Delivered | Delivery Date | |
	Ordered	Delivered		First	Last
Curtiss A. and M. Corp.	A800–A815	A800–A814	15	Jan. 4/18	May 27/18
Curtiss A. and M. Corp	A1549–A1819	A1549–A1819	271	April 12/18	July 9/18
	Subtotal		286		
LWF Engineering Corp.	A1099–A1350	A1099–A1398 [2]	253	June 15/18	Feb. 21/19
Standard Aircraft Corp.	A1399–A1440	A1399–A1440	42	June 22/18	Oct. 4/18
	Total Curtiss HS-1Ls		581		

Production of Curtiss HS-2L flying boats[3]

| Manufacturer | Serial Numbers | | Quantity Delivered | Delivery Date | |
	Ordered	Delivered		First	Last
Curtiss A. and M. Corp.	A1820–A2207	A1820–A2207	388	July 15/18	Dec. 27/18
Standard Aircraft Corp.	A1441–A1548	A1441–A1578	138	Oct. 12/18	Jan. –/19
Gallaudet Aircraft Corp.	A2217–A2276	A2217–A2276	60	Aug. 19/18	Feb. –/19
Loughead Aircraft Mfg. Co.	A4228–A4229	A4228–A4229	2	Jan. 5/19	Jan. 5/19
Boeing Airplane Co.	A4231–A4255	A4231–A4255	25	Feb. 8/19	June 8/19
Assembled by USN from spares					
At Miami, Fla.	A5564–A5569	A5564–A5569	6	Jan. –/19	Feb. –/19
At Hampton Roads, Va.	A5615–A5618	A5615–A5618	4	Feb. –/19	Feb. –/20
At Key West, Fla.	A5787	A5787	1	Nov. –/19	–
At Anacostia, D.C.	A5808	A5808	1	Feb. –/20	–
At Coco Solo, C.Z.	A6506	A6506	1	Oct. 4/22	–
At NAF Phil., Pa.	A6507–A6513	A6507–A6513	7	Nov. –/22	Jan. –/24
At San Diego, Calif.	A6553–A6556	A6553–A6556	4	Oct. 6/22	Oct. 6/22
	Total Curtiss HS-2Ls		637		

Total production of Curtiss HS-1L and HS-2L flying boats – 1 218

Notes

1.   While all aircraft delivered are listed as HS-1Ls in USN records, many and probably most of the surviving machines would have been converted to HS-2L standards. Conversions are not listed in the records.

2.   Forty-seven aircraft with the following serial numbers were cancelled and not delivered: A1116, A1134, A1148, A1192, A1220, A1222, A1228, A1234, A1272, A1277, A1278, A1287, A1289, A1290, A1309, A1313, A1314, A1319, A1323, A1325, A1328–A1350, A1366, A1380, A1388, and A1394.

    Some aircraft were not delivered consecutively by serial number, so the last serial was not necessarily the last aircraft delivered.

3.   Some hulls, the most labour intensive component, were subcontracted out by at least two main contractors to expedite production. The subcontractors identified their hulls with nameplates and were known to have been erroneously listed as makers of the complete aircraft, as follows:

    Curtiss's subcontractors: Niagara Motor Boat Co., Niagara Falls, N.Y.; Mathews Boat Co., Port Clinton, Ohio.

    LWF's subcontractors: College Point Boat Works, College Point, N.Y.; George Lawley Co., Boston, Mass.; Mathews Boat Co., Port Clinton, Ohio.

HS-3 had a completely new hull design, conceived by the NAF and based on their earlier hull design for the F-5L. The wings, which were a slight extension of the HS-2L wings, used upper-wing ailerons only, like the Boeing-built HS-2Ls, and new tail surfaces were fitted. Four HS-3s were completed in 1919 by Curtiss Engineering, serial numbers A5459–A5462, and two more in 1920 by the NAF, serial num-

The HS-3L A5459 with new hull, new wing-tip floats, new tail, over-wing exhausts, and increased wingspan – a completely new design. (GHCM)

bers A5590–A5591. The record cards note dissatisfaction with all six machines – five were scrapped by 1922, and one was stored and scrapped the following year.

In the postwar years several civil conversions of the HS-2L were made in Canada and the United States. Military aircraft are seldom suitable for immediate civil use; they are designed to carry guns and

Aero Ltd.'s civil conversion of the HS-2L, the first such conversion made. S.A. (Al) Cheesman (right) later became a well-known pilot, experienced in the bush, the Arctic and the Antarctic. C.A. (Duke) Schiller (far left in water) also became a well-known and colourful bush pilot. (S.A. Cheesman)

NAM's specimen shows the seating arrangement of the five-place Canadian civil HS-2L. (K.M. Molson)

A typical U.S. six-place open-cockpit HS-2L conversion by Aeromarine designated as their Model 85. (NASM A5114)

This seven-place HS-2L operated by Pacific Airways Co. was similar to few other seven-place machines, though its front cockpit was probably larger than most. Pilot Ansel Eckmann is in the rear cockpit on the left side. (J. Eckmann, B. Eckmann)

bombs – heavy compact items – while civil aircraft carry people and freight, which require more room.

The first HS-2Ls to enter civilian use served briefly in their original form but were soon modified. Aero Ltd. made, or had made, the first conversion in late 1919 or early 1920. Aero's version had a large communal cockpit, and the crew seats, controls, and instruments were moved forward. It also had an exhaust system arranged to conduct the exhaust gases forward and above the wing, possibly an idea borrowed from the Curtiss HS-3. Aero's version established the six-place conversion as the American standard, but it was one of only a few to have a communal cockpit and no other is known to have an over-wing exhaust. It is surprising that the latter feature was not adopted by others since it surely must have provided some noise relief for both passengers and crew.

The next conversion was made in Canada in 1920, when the Air Board prepared drawings for a five-place conversion that added a single side-by-side cockpit between the nose cockpit and the pilot's cockpit. This arrangement was adopted by all Canadian operators. A few operators later enlarged the front cockpit for convenience. No six-place conversions were made in Canada because it is now believed the deterioration of performance with the extra load would have prevented issuance of a certificate of airworthiness.

In 1921 the Aeromarine Plane & Motor Co. of Keyport, New Jersey, entered into an agreement with the USN for the marketing of both F-5L and HS-2L flying boats. Aeromarine widely advertised and

promoted an unmodified HS-2L at $6160; priced a six-place, open-cockpit version of the HS-2L, designated their Model 85, at $6500; and priced a six-place cabin version, designated their Model 80, at $9000. Their model designations were not normally used.

The prototype of Aeromarine's cabin conversion of the HS-2L, their Model 80. A raised crew location is at the back of the cabin. Secretary of the Navy, Edwin Denby, is boarding for a flight over Washington, D.C. (NASM 86-5717)

The Aeromarine six-place, open-cockpit version had the original nose cockpit filled in and two side-by-side cockpits fitted closely in front of the standard pilot's cockpit. This general arrangement became the usual American civil HS-2L version. Only a few were actually made by Aeromarine, probably for economic reasons mainly, but possibly also because individuals of small private companies could convert Navy HS-2Ls more cheaply and could readily introduce their special features.

There were many variants of the general six-place arrangement. A few had a communal cockpit for six, and a few had an additional single cockpit cut in the nose. In the latter case it is likely the seven places would be filled only on short joy rides, and with reduced fuel loads. A few with communal cockpits had flight controls and crew seats moved forward. All these variations could easily be made in the United States, where there were no airworthiness requirements to be met, no drawings to be approved, no inspectors to be satisfied.

The prototype of the Aeromarine cabin version was officially launched about May 2, 1921, at Anacostia Air Station, by Edwin Denby, Secretary of the Navy, in the presence of other dignitaries; shortly afterward, Denby and others flew the aircraft over Washington, D.C. The prototype seated four passengers in the front part of the cabin and the crew of two in a raised open cockpit at the back. The aircraft was sold in 1922 to Great Lakes Airways. From available information it seems that only two examples of this cabin version were made. The second one was modified and the crew seats

Douglas Co. made the second of two cabin-version HS-2Ls ever built. Its crew has been moved to the front of the cabin. Its radiator is partially blanked off; the bow bears the marine registration number 973-A and the name Gail. *(Harry Gann)*

were moved forward in the cabin. It was made by the Douglas Co. (later, Douglas Aircraft Co.) in Los Angeles. It was modified from Boeing-built HS-2L A4251 to Aeromarine drawings for Pacific Marine Airways.

The final HS-2L conversion began late in 1927 and the prototype first flew on May 11, 1928. It was the only conversion featuring improved aerodynamics; all others were concerned only with passenger and crew accommodation. This conversion was designed and built by Canadian Vickers Ltd. of Montreal at the request of Canadian Airways (old) and consisted of fitting new two-bay wings with

A Canadian Vickers HS-3L at Sept-Îles, Quebec. Only three of this version were made. (NAM)

an improved airfoil to the usual Canadian five-place, open-cockpit hull. Canadian Vickers then designated the type the Curtiss HS-3L, apparently unaware the designation had been used before. It had also been named the Canadian Carrier. Now, to avoid confusion, it is commonly called the Canadian Vickers HS-3L Canadian Carrier. It achieved an improved climb-and-takeoff performance as probably desired.

Performance figures are given in Part III for the Canadian Vickers HS-3L Canadian Carrier, but no figures are available for other civil conversions. However, it is easy to speculate about their performance. Probably the five-place Canadian version would have had a performance almost identical to that of the original USN HS-2L – not very sprightly. The six-place, open-cockpit conversion's performance would have deteriorated somewhat, possibly to the point that it would not meet Canadian airworthiness requirements. Had it met them, this version would surely have been used in Canada. The Aeromarine six-place cabin conversion would likely have suffered increased weight and, probably drag, with a consequent decrease in performance. This being the case, and considering the cabin conversion's higher price, it is not surprising that only two were made.

Actual Performance and Handling Characteristics

The performance achieved in actual service by some early aircraft varied from that achieved in initial tests. There could have been a variety of reasons, but a prime one was that the HS-2L and other early flying boats had wooden hulls, and many were large and difficult to hoist out of the water. If a machine was based at a large and well-equipped station, it would be removed from the water regularly, given a chance to dry out, and thus not suffer too much. However, a machine that remained in the water for extended periods got heavier and heavier and its performance became decidedly sluggish, particularly toward the end of the flying season. In Canada, many machines would be in the water almost continuously when not airborne, from about May 1 to November 1.

When talking with former HS-2L pilots in Canada there was never any mention of the machine having vices, nor do Canadian accident records indicate such proneness. Usually what would come up in conversation was the fact that the machine was very heavy on the controls, and that in rough weather both crew members had to work on them to keep the airplane under control. But the heaviness

An OPAS HS-2L docking. Crewmen wait for the pilot's signal to help steer the aircraft by causing the wing-float to enter the water. (E.J. Cooper)

seemed to be taken for granted in a large flying boat. The fact that the HS-2L was difficult to control on the water was also often mentioned. This was due both to its large sail area and, like all water-based aircraft of its period, the absence of water rudders. Consequently it was greatly at the mercy of currents and winds. It was common practice in Canada for one or two crew members to climb onto the lower wing when taxiing in confined areas or approaching a dock. Here they would wait for a signal from the pilot to move out on one wing or the other. This would immerse one wingtip float in the water and help make a turn in the desired direction.

It is fortunate that Ontario Provincial Air Service (OPAS) pilot Terrance B. Tully wrote an unpublished report in 1926 outlining the normal operating procedures for HS-2Ls. It gives a good idea of how the machine was actually flown on forestry patrols. (Tully was lost on a transatlantic flight attempt in September 1927.) Some excerpts from his report follow.

> A large flying boat requires, as a general rule, a fairly large lake
> to alight in to permit taking off again and getting high enough

for safety before making a turn or getting over the land. This eliminates many lakes that would make good landing grounds for a smaller machine with a quicker take off and better climb than an HS-2L. In the warmer weather of July and August when the HS-2L is heavily laden it often takes a mile [1.6 km] or more before leaving the water and owing to the humidity the climb is very slow so a lake of 3 to 5 miles [4.8 to 8 km] in length and at least a mile [1.6 km] or more in width is necessary for the comfortable handling of the machine. The time taken to reach an altitude sufficiently high to start a patrol varies considerably with weather conditions but the average rate of climb with full load is about 3,000 ft [900 m] in 30 minutes. There have been occasions when machines have not reached that height within an hour.

Although an HS-2L has reached an altitude of 8,000 ft [2 400 m] its best average height is about 4,000 ft [1 200 m] with its effective operating load. In consequence, the HS-2L on patrol is always flying at its maximum service ceiling. This is very essential in the interests of safety as the higher the machine is flying the better the chance of gliding to a lake to make a forced landing and, also, the farther the range of vision for observation purposes. The HS-2L is comparatively slow as its average speed is about 65 mph [105 km/hr]. The machine has a steep gliding angle and the speed necessary to maintain good maneuvering control without the engine is slightly more than the average level speed with the engine on. Owing to the steep gliding angle and low serviceable ceiling of the machine the margin of safety maintained is governed by the route followed to ensure remaining in gliding distance of a lake. This very often means long detours to avoid dry country and, of course, an unavoidable waste of fuel and time.

It is necessary to carry an air engineer on operations particularly owing to the size and unwieldiness of the HS-2L on the water and the difficulty in approaching and tying up to docks or shorelines in awkward wind conditions.

In 1926 the OPAS was in the process of changing over its HS-2L fleet to high-compression 400 hp Liberty engines. This involved fitting high-compression pistons during the next engine overhaul, which OPAS was carrying out every 80 flying hours at that time. The writer is not aware of any other operator making this change-over, but there well may have been others. Fortunately, Tully has included some impressions of the improvements brought about by high-compression pistons:

The HS-2L has been improved by the installation of the high compression Liberty engine. The take off is then very fair – the average being from 400 to 600 yds [360 to 550 m]. Its rate of climb is roughly 200 ft/min [60 m/min] with normal load. Its service ceiling is about 4,500 ft [1 400 m] and its absolute ceiling is about 6,500 ft [2 000 m]. Its cruising speed is 65 mph [105 km/hr] and its top speed at ground level is 70 mph [110 km/hr].

The engine as originally installed in the HS-1L and HS-2L. Oil tanks are slung on both sides from the engine bearer. (CF PL1443815)

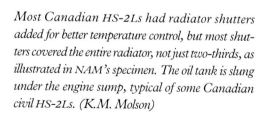

Most Canadian HS-2Ls had radiator shutters added for better temperature control, but most shutters covered the entire radiator, not just two-thirds, as illustrated in NAM's specimen. The oil tank is slung under the engine sump, typical of some Canadian civil HS-2Ls. (K.M. Molson)

Tully's comments bring out the difficulties of flying the HS-2L from the pilot's viewpoint. However, from the ground crew's viewpoint its large size and unwieldiness made it awkward to handle and look after. Its large and heavy engine, installed between the wings, was difficult to access for service and even more so for an engine change. Some of these problems may best be grasped by looking at the two photographs showing an engine change and hull repairs being made in the bush. What the photographs do not show are the hordes of mosquitoes and black flies that invariably hover around anyone working in the bush.

Having just learned that the HS-2L was known in Canada as a rather slow, stodgy, but viceless "old lady," the reader will now be surprised to learn that in the USN it had acquired a "Jekyll-and-Hyde" reputation for a time. The respected Edward P. Warner, after retiring as Assistant Secretary of the Navy, became editor of *Aviation* magazine, and almost immediately wrote a brief editorial in 1929 under the title "The Paradox Plane":

> The most dangerous plane in the Navy has by far the best safety record. The planes of the HS-2L type are pusher flying boats powered with a Liberty engine. They are unstable longitudinally and are apt to slip off on a wing without warning. They go into a spin easily and are next to impossible to get out. They are decidedly underpowered and the Navy in 1923 branded

An engine change after a forced landing in the bush called for hard work and ingenuity. This one occurred in 1921, following an engine failure in Air Board HS-2L G-CYAH. (G.R. Hutt)

Laurentide Co. HS-2L G-CAAD /A1878 beached for hull repairs on a Quebec lake in 1921. (Source unknown)

them as too dangerous for any violent maneuvers, yet this type of plane, during the last three years when it was in use, was flown nearly thirty thousand hours or over two million miles [3 000 000 km] without a fatal accident.

Several lessons can be drawn from this paradox. In the first place it shows that accident statistics must be studied with considerable care and diligence. In the second place it shows that a good safety record depends on careful operation held within the limits of what a plane is capable of doing [and what it was designed to do]. The HS-2Ls, after they were pronounced as dangerous, were used only for patrol and cruising work under favorable conditions. They did not take part in any maneuvers that necessitated anything but straight flying. The third conclusion applies to pilots. As one Navy man put it, "All good HS-2L pilots were killed off by 1923 and therefore there were no more accidents."

This sounds like another paradox but it is not. What he meant was that there were a certain group of pilots who had become very expert in the handling of the boats. They threw them around as only an unstable plane can be thrown around, but the plane was "tricky" and every so often a pilot would not pull out.

HS-2L record cards bear out this last assertion: 11 machines spun out between April 1919 and September 1921, doubtless in most cases with disastrous consequences for the crews. Another proof of the old adage "There are old pilots and bold pilots, but no old, bold pilots."

Capt. Wm. P. Wishar of the United States Coast Guard (USCG), as quoted in Pearcy's *A History of U.S. Coast Guard Aviation*, comments on HS-2L spinning characteristics:

> The plane we had as our 'work horse' was the Navy HS-2L flying boat. It was a heavy plane; single engine (Liberty), pusher-type, open cockpit. It was staunchly built, could land in a fairly heavy sea when emergency demanded and could take off in a moderate sea. It took off at a speed of 48 knots [89 km/hr] and flew at 55 knots [102 km/hr], a leeway of 7 knots [13 km/hr] between flying speed and stalling speed. If she stalled, she went into a spin. No flyer that I've heard of ever pulled a fully manned and equipped HS-2L out of a spin....
>
> Speaking of 'spinning' an H boat: Lieutenant Robert Donohue, believed the HS-2L *could* be brought out of a spin. One day* at the Morehead City Air Station, he had all removable gear and weights removed from an HS-2L (such as anchor and anchor line, sea-anchor, mooring lines, water casks, emergency gas can, tools, etc.), and with a moderate amount of gas and only himself in the plane, took off. I had not known of his intention. When he was in the air, someone told me he was going to try a spin. I would not have permitted it had I known.... Donohue climbed to about 3,500 feet [1100 m] then deliberately put the HS-2L into a spin as we watched helplessly – expecting a crash.... I didn't know whether he should have a court-martial for risking the plane and his life or be recommended for a medal for bravery beyond the call of duty. He retired as Rear Admiral.

---

* This must have been in 1921 or later, as Wishar took over the Morehead Air Station only then.

Chapter 3

THE HS-1L AND HS-2L

IN WORLD WAR I SERVICE

German submarines had been active since the beginning of World War I. The USN would have been well aware of this. However, the growing capability of submarines was brought home to the Navy in 1916 by two visits of the unarmed commercial submarine *Deutschland*. The first was to Baltimore, Maryland, July 2 to August 1, and the second was to New London, Connecticut, October 31 to November 21. In both cases the *Deutschland* brought, and returned with, cargoes of useful materials. Between these visits the U-53 dropped in unannounced to Newport, Rhode Island, delivered messages, stayed three hours, and departed saying it had no need to take on

HS-1Ls at L'Aber Vrach NAS, 1918. HS-1Ls tended to predominate in France. The station aircraft identification on hulls and upper wings is well shown here. (USNA)

supplies. The next day, the U-53 sank six ships just off the coast – four British, one Dutch, and one Norwegian – with no loss of life.

In February 1917 the USN established eight naval air stations along the east coast, including one in the Canal Zone (C.Z.) to protect the Panama Canal. After the declaration of war on Germany in April the USN decided it would also have to set up naval air stations in Europe to protect both troop and supply ships. By war's end the USN had established 21 naval air stations overseas, 13 in France, 1 in England, 5 in Ireland, and 2 in Italy – of which 11 only, all in France, would have HS-1L/HS-2L aircraft. In addition, the U.S. Marine Corps operated an HS-1L/HS-2L station in the Azores.

HS-1Ls at Tréguier NAS, 1918, bearing station aircraft numbers T7, T6, and T5. Note the different style and location of these numbers compared with those used at L'Aber Vrach NAS. (USNA)

The eleven French stations are listed in the following table in the order of their commissioning dates. Station identification was displayed prominently with the station aircraft number on the sides of the hull, on the top of the upper wing, and, possibly, on the underside of the lower wing. Only the patrol stations were assigned identification letters.

All HS-1Ls and HS-2Ls were shipped to Pauillac, France, for assembly and test flying and distribution to the stations. The first eight HS-1Ls arrived there on May 24, 1918, and the first was flown on June 11. Judging by figures shown for machines on hand on November 11, it is possible that incoming aircraft were not cleared quickly. Of the total 149 machines on hand, 80 (approximately 54 per cent) were at Pauillac. Also, of the 235 recorded as being shipped

Commissioning Date	Naval Air Station (identification letters)	Function	HS-1L/HS-2L a/c allowance	HS-1L/HS-2L on hand Nov. 11/18
Aug. 31/17	Le Moutic	training	not established	11
Oct. 17/17	Brest (BA)	patrol	–	16★
Nov. 27/17	Le Croisic (C, later LC)	patrol	24	1★
Dec. 1/17	Pauillac	assembly & repair	–	80★
Mar. 14/18	Île-Trudy (I)	patrol	24	19★
June 4/18	L'Aber Vrach (LV)			
June 8/18	Arcachon (A)	patrol	–	7
June 14/18	St. Trojan (ST)	patrol	24	7
Nov. 1/18	Tréguier (T)	patrol	18	8

★ These HS-1Ls and HS-2Ls were supplemented by other types.

HS-1Ls and HS-2Ls at Brest NAS in 1918. HS-2Ls are first and third from the right. Note their larger rudders and balance areas. (USNA)

overseas, 86 were unaccounted for and were presumably still en route, or written off, as of November 11.

No HS-1L or HS-2L is known to have sunk a submarine, although some were claimed as having done so at the time. However, this is not surprising: few submarines were claimed sunk by Allied

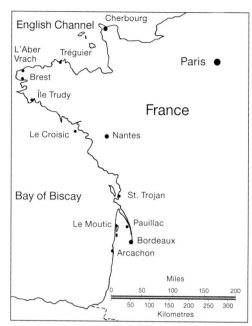

Locations of USN air stations in France during World War I. (K.M. Molson)

HS-1Ls at Le Moutic NAS training base, 1918. (USNA)

aircraft during World War I, and still fewer of these were found to be valid kills postwar when claims were checked with enemy records. However, it is claimed, probably correctly, that no Allied ship was lost while being escorted by either a lighter-than-air or heavier-than-air aerial patrol. Aerial patrols seem to have served their intended purpose.

The first French stations were established well before HS-1Ls arrived. However, beginning as early as September 1917, the USN obtained, apparently on loan, a number of F.B.A., Tellier, G. Levy, and Donnet light flying boats from France. This enabled training operations to begin – not only with flight training but also with familiarization training in the area and patrol organization. The first USN aerial patrol ventured from Le Croisic Naval Air Station (NAS) on November 18, 1917, with Tellier flying boats – nine days before the station was officially commissioned. The Marine Base in the Azores was established on January 21, 1918, at Ponta Delgada, and began training with Curtiss R-6 twin-float seaplanes. These were the first U.S.-built aircraft to serve American forces overseas. Later HS-1Ls and HS-2Ls were shipped there directly, not through Pauillac.

All patrol stations indicated above were assigned routine patrol areas that were monitored regularly for enemy activity. In addition, convoy patrols were carried out as required to protect shipping, and special submarine patrols were sent to check activities reported by any source. As already noted, the first patrol along the French coast was carried out from Le Croisic on November 18, 1917. A total of 4314 patrols had been carried out when the last one was made from Brest on December 18, 1918, on the occasion of President Woodrow Wilson's visit to France.

Aircraft from the six patrol stations listed above sighted twenty-seven submarines while on patrol. They attacked twenty-five of them, and are believed to have damaged twelve and thought to have sunk four. Also, the American experience corresponded to that of the other Allies in that no ship was lost while under aerial escort. In addition, it is recorded in the USN patrol area that until the spring of 1918, an average of one ship a day was lost. However, in the last ten months of the year, only three ships were lost – an indication of the effectiveness of the Franco-American patrols.

At the end of World War I, no HS-1Ls or HS-2Ls in Europe were returned to the United States. All were scrapped except for four in the Azores that were given to Portugal. This made good economic sense since surplus aircraft of all sorts were readily available to all of the Allies.

As mentioned earlier, the setting up of east coast naval air stations was authorized early in 1917. Following the declaration of war by the United States, the number of stations was increased and included two in Canada. Canada had no air service then; it was agreed that a Royal Canadian Naval Air Service would be established and, until it became operational, the USN would operate stations at Dartmouth, near Halifax, Nova Scotia, and at North Sidney, Nova Scotia on Cape Breton Island. An additional station in Newfoundland was still being considered at the war's end.

These stations varied in size, and the largest were those protecting the major shipping centres of New York (with 75 per cent of the traffic) and Baltimore. These stations, Rockaway NAS and Hampton Roads NAS, were by far the largest, and were supported by smaller stations to the north and south. The main equipment of all stations was the Curtiss HS-1L/HS-2L flying boat; the larger stations usually had one or two twin-engine flying boats, and some also had non-rigid dirigibles and captive balloons. However, as in France, many stations were ready before the HS-1Ls and HS-2Ls came off the production lines, so Curtiss R-6 or R-6L twin-float seaplanes were used for both flight training and patrol familiarization until the flying boats became available.

Naval air stations were established at all of the following locations (listed geographically from north to south along the North American east coast): North Sidney, N.S.; Dartmouth, N.S.; Chatham, Mass.; New London, Conn.; Montauk, L.I., N.Y.; Bay Shore, L.I., N.Y.; Rockaway, L.I., N.Y.; Brooklyn, N.Y.; Cape May, N.J.; Anacostia, Washington, D.C.; Hampton Roads, Va.; Norfolk, Va.; Morehead City, N.C.; Brunswick, Ga.*; Miami, Fla.; Key West, Fla.; Coco Solo, C.Z.

All of the above stations' primary functions were coastal patrol and aerial protection to shipping, except for Anacostia and Hampton Roads.

Anacostia was a repair station and Hampton Roads, in addition to being a patrol station, acted as a training centre for both flight and ground crew until May 1918, and served as an experimental station for both aircraft and aeronautical equipment.

HS-2Ls A1386, A1833 and A135 at San Diego NAS, 1918. This was the only naval air station on the U.S. west coast at that time. (Boeing– W. & A. Fawver HS 3641)

Other than the stations noted, there were only two in the United States in 1918, one at Pensacola, Florida, and the other at San Diego, California. Pensacola NAS was established on the Gulf of Mexico prior to the war and was known as the Naval Aeronautic Station Pensacola until December 1917, when it became the Pensacola NAS. It was the main USN aviation training centre and has continued in that role up to the present. In 1918 Pensacola acquired a large number of

---

* This station was just being established in early November 1918, so it never actually operated.

HS-1Ls and HS-2Ls and continued using them for a variety of training purposes until 1927. San Diego was the main base for the Pacific Fleet, and the San Diego NAS was established there in August 1918, then equipped primarily with HS-2Ls.

A brief description of Rockaway and Hampton Roads, the largest and most interesting stations, follows and focuses primarily on their HS-1L/HS-2L operations. Operations of the other stations were similar to those of the larger stations but on a smaller scale. The smaller stations, when located nearby, were frequently called upon to assist in the larger stations' operations.

Rockaway NAS was located on Jamaica Bay on the west end of Long Island and close to the Port of New York. It was authorized in May 1917, and construction of separate hangars for the seaplanes and non-rigid dirigibles as well as shops and barracks began shortly afterward. By November 11, 1918, its complement was 125 officers and 1160 men. In June 1918 there were 29 seaplanes in use, and on November 11, 1918, 18 seaplanes, 2 non-rigid dirigibles, and 4 captive balloons were in daily use.

The patrol area originally extended east along Long Island for about 225 km (140 mi.) and followed the New Jersey coast south for about 112 km (70 mi.). Later the area was extended and, according to Lt. Charles F. Matthews, the HS boats "not infrequently prolonged their flights to sea for 100 miles [160 km] and covered 8,000 square miles [20 700 km²]." The early patrol flights were made by Curtiss R-6 tractor twin-float seaplanes, and the first patrol from Rockaway was made on November 7, 1917. Daily flights were made, weather and ice conditions permitting. After the arrival of the HS boats and once the pilots became familiar with them, patrols were extended and increased. In August 1918 a "spider web" system of patrols began, following the pattern developed at RNAS Felixstowe Station in England. In addition, the patrols carried out a large amount of escort work for European convoys leaving New York, as well as for coastal shipping and especially for ships of unusual value.

On August 24 two HS-2Ls on patrol duty collided in heavy fog near Fire Island Lightship. One machine, A1273, spun in. While the other landed safely, it was not able to find any of the crew of A1273 despite a careful search of the wreckage. Apparently no machine from Rockaway made contact with a submarine.

Rockaway was the base for the large NC flying boats, and the prototype, the NC-1, was first flown there on October 4, 1918. Three NC boats left there on May 7, 1919, and one of them, the NC-4, reached England on May 31 via Newfoundland, the Azores, and Portugal to complete the first transatlantic flight.

The Hampton Roads NAS was an offshoot of the Curtiss Aviation School at Newport News, Virginia, which had been in operation since 1915. In May 1917, 17 student aviators were sent there by the USN. In August, two naval officers were sent to the Curtiss School to take over the Navy's training operations there. The new naval air station was formed at Norfolk, across Hampton Roads from Newport News. It was at the entrance to Chesapeake Bay on the shipping route to Baltimore, the second busiest port on the east coast after New York. Navy personnel and equipment were moved to the new site on August 28. The seaplanes were initially moored out for two weeks until the canvas hangars were erected, marking the beginning of the Hampton Roads NAS.

In due course, aircraft hangars, barracks and shops were built, as well as a non-rigid dirigible hangar and hydrogen plant. By December 1 the unit had been granted the full status of an NAS. By November 11, 1918, the station roster comprised 176 officers and 1 227 men, the largest station on the east coast. By April 1, 1918, there were 22 machines of 8 types at the station, and by November 11 there were 65 machines of 11 types, along with 1 dirigible and 15 captive balloons, of which only 4 or 5 were inflated at one time.

Instruction continued through to May 1918, but was interrupted for a month in winter when Hampton Roads was frozen over from shore to shore – a most unusual occurrence. In addition to aviators, some dirigible pilots and captive-balloon pilots as well as many ground crew were trained. Training at Hampton Roads stopped in May 1918, when the USN training system was reorganized.

Patrols from Hampton Roads extended north from Cape Henry at the mouth of Chesapeake Bay for about 180 km (110 mi.) and then turned south to follow the 183-m (100-fathom) line for about 200 km (125 mi.), bringing the patrol to a point about 185 km (115 mi.) off the North Carolina coast. The patrol would turn west to the coast, then north along the coast to Cape Henry. Later, when refuelling stations were established, it was possible to extend patrols; after Morehead NAS was established, a further extension was possible. To cover this large area and to escort convoys leaving Norfolk, an average of 18 seaplanes, largely single- or twin-engine flying boats, were required from June to September. This was increased to 28 and, later, to 30 machines. Also, all convoys operating within range of the station had to be escorted by at least two aircraft. As well, emergency calls had to be answered by stand-by machines ready to respond.

In Matthews' account the only apparent submarine contact made by a Hampton Roads machine occurred on July 21, when Curtiss R-6L A961, piloted by Ensign C.B. Burke, located an object that "appeared to be a submerged submarine." A 45-kg (100-lb) bomb was dropped; it exploded and the object disappeared. This mission was reported to the station, and a two-plane patrol of Curtiss H-12s was sent out. The patrol found an oil slick but determined nothing definite. There was only one other submarine contact made by the east coast patrol stations. This occurred on July 21, 1918, when Ensign E. Lingard of Gloucester, Massachusetts, and the crew of HS-1L A1695 received word at Chatham NAS that a submarine was firing on a tug and barges. The crew first spotted the burning boats, then the submarine firing on the boats, and they dove over the submarine. The bomb-release did not work. They made a second pass, and Chief Mechanic Howard managed to release the bomb manually. The bomb landed within a few feet of the U-boat but failed to explode. A second HS-1L, piloted by Capt. P.B. Eaton, found the submarine and dropped a bomb that also failed to explode.★ Afterward it was said the bombs were so close that, had they exploded, the U-boat would have been sunk or badly damaged. Other machines were soon on the scene; they searched all day but turned up nothing.

Some American writers have said this was the only incident in which a surfaced U-boat was attacked by seaplanes in U.S. waters. At the request of the City of Gloucester, who wanted to commemorate the incident, the Navy Department presented the community with the hull of A1695 in 1919. It was intended that the hull would be enclosed in a transparent casing and placed upon a granite shaft at the entrance to Gloucester Harbor. This was not done. The hull was paraded through the streets of Gloucester and turned over to the park commissioners. Inquiries today indicate that the hull no longer exists.

While these were the only two occasions on which a submarine was spotted, there were numerous other occasions when aircraft were sent out to search for a reported submarine, only to find "the submarine" was some other object or simply not locatable.

In September refuelling stations had been established for the patrols, and HS flying boats could extend their daily patrols to six or eight hours each day.

The Experimental Department at Hampton Roads carried out a wide variety of tasks. These included tests of complete aircraft to assess their performance. The prototype of the HS-1L A800, the modified HS-1L A1599 with wing extensions (the precursor of the HS-2L), and other new machines such as the Curtiss L-2 triplane and Boeing C were among those tested.

The Department also made a large number of radio tests. These included different types of sets transmitting both code and voice, installations in various aircraft types, different antennas, and different helmets for the crew. The tests were felt to be most successful and resulted in considerable improvements. Various lights for

★ These bombs, Clarke Mk IVs of 54 kg (120 lb) apiece, were giving the USN constant trouble at this time.

night flying were tried, as well as searchlights. Also, there were tests of bomb sights and parachutes, and experiments with kite balloons.

Armament tests were also made, including trials of the Davis gun. Little has been said about this unusual weapon so further comment, as taken from Matthews' account, will be of interest here. It was reported "two HS-2Ls ... are equipped with Davis guns but so far [it] has not been possible to obtain very satisfactory results...." Again, on October 25 the following comments were made:

> [T]wo HS-2Ls were sent out on a routine patrol with Davis guns. They were equipped as prescribed with 70 lb [30 kg] of sand in the tail and two experienced pilots. They completed a patrol of approximately 4 hours but experienced great difficulty in handling. Both pilots report that the gun not only made the machine exceedingly nose heavy and severely impaired the visibility of the pilots but also made the planes "cranky." Apparently the added weight and wind resistance hindered dangerously the correction of bumps and made it difficult to take the aircraft in and out of turns. It is not believed that this gun is practicable for use in HS type seaplanes.

In contrast to this Hampton Roads' finding on the Davis gun in the HS-2L, the Key West NAS reported the following, according to Matthews:

> Several tests were made with the Davis non-recoil gun at Key West. On one occasion six shots were fired at an old steel wreck in the harbor which served as a target. Of these six shots four were direct hits, made by an inexperienced officer. The performance showed the ease with which the Davis gun can be operated accurately. It functioned perfectly but due to faulty ammunition was not absolutely satisfactory as a tracer. No shock was felt in the boat* following the firing of the gun and there was no danger of the buckshot, which takes up the recoil, damaging the plane. One of the shots upon striking a metal girder exploded, damaging the target.

The results of the two tests were so divergent that it is difficult to understand them unless there were unknown factors involved, ones not mentioned in the quoted results.

In early November, 1918, Hampton Roads was assigned to operate a daily mail service to Anacostia NAS (Curtiss HS-2Ls) and a similar service to the Yorktown Naval Base until the Atlantic Fleet was moved from there.

---

* The type of flying boat is not specified, but the Curtiss HS-1L and HS-2L were the only ones in use at Key West NAS.

Chapter 4

THE HS-2L AFTER

WORLD WAR I

Immediately after the signing of the Armistice, most USN patrol stations on the east coast were closed, the personnel were discharged, and the aircraft were moved to some of the main stations. Hampton Roads, near Norfolk, Virginia, was the main collecting point, but others were Miami, Florida, and the Brooklyn Navy Yard.

The first USN sale of surplus machines was made by auction in September 1919, but others followed. Sale by auction was, apparently, the preferred USN method of disposing surplus equipment. However, Aeromarine and Motor Co. obtained a Felixstowe F-5L★ in February 1920 and converted it to civil use as the Aeromarine 75. Aeromarine was convinced there was a civilian market for both F-5Ls and Curtiss HS-2Ls and attempted to get the USN to let Aeromarine be the exclusive agent for the two machine types. The USN, while reluctant, was persuaded. Aeromarine took a two-page spread in the *New York Times* and *Aviation* magazine in early 1921 advertising the HS-2L, and soon after made sales tours with an HS-2L. However, few HS-2Ls were sold by Aeromarine and it lost its monopoly. No F-5Ls were sold.

Aeromarine's proposal to the USN was that it would buy options for 135 HS-2Ls at $100 each and pay a further $2 000 each when Aeromarine sold them. Apparently only 125 were acquired. Aeromarine's price for an unmodified HS-2L was, as mentioned earlier, $6 160. Examples could soon be bought directly from the USN and from aircraft dealers more cheaply. The largest dealer was E. Epstein, doing business as the Southland Jobbing House at Norfolk, Virginia, who in 1924 was said to be taking "65 hydroplanes" from the USN, probably mostly HS-2Ls. F.G. Ericson of Baltimore, Maryland, and Toronto also dealt in HS-2Ls, as did others. The price of HS-2Ls dropped quickly, as can be seen in the *U.S. Air Services*

★ The Felixstowe F.5 was designed at Felixstowe, England, by John Porte (the F indicating Felixstowe; all Curtiss twin-engine boats were H boats). The F.5 was selected by the USN in 1918, and the U.S. NAF installed the Liberty engines and modified the hull construction but not the lines. However, these machines are widely referred to in the United States as Curtiss F-5Ls. The NAF built 137, Curtiss built 60, and Canadian Aeroplanes Ltd. built 30.

advertisement, but the Liberty engine remained in aeronautical and marine use longer, so its price did not drop as quickly.

The wartime costs of HS-2Ls to the U.S. government are shown for comparison. Larger contractors with large orders could produce machines more cheaply than smaller ones, so prices varied. The costs below are for airframe without engine, instruments, or armament.

Company	Quantity	Rounded cost per aircraft
Curtiss	673	$11 000
LWF	250	$13 000
Standard	80	$15 000
Gallaudet	60	$14 750

Average price per aircraft $12 000

Prices were determined on a "cost plus 12 per cent" basis for Curtiss and on "cost plus 15 per cent" for other makers – plus a bonus

This advertisement announced the first postwar sale of HS-2Ls. (Aerial Age Weekly, September 15, 1919)

This advertisement, undoubtedly aimed at rum-runners, indicates that new HS-2Ls and Liberty engines were still readily available in February 1927. (Aviation, February 7, 1927)

for costs under a bogie of $13 000. Cost figures are from a U.S. government memorandum of May 22, 1919. The number of aircraft attributed to makers varies slightly from the actual number made.

There were a good many HS-2Ls sold, but in the absence of civil aviation records in the United States prior to 1927, it is not possible to determine the number, get an indication of the use to which the machines were put, or discover to which countries they might have been exported. Nevertheless it is suspected that a sizable number were used as rumrunners along the Florida coast, as described in Chapter 5 in excerpts taken from the meagre available accounts.

After the United States, Canada operated the largest number of Curtiss HS-2Ls in the postwar years. This is not surprising. With its many lakes and rivers and large unsettled areas, Canada needed water-based aircraft that could carry a sizable load. The Canadian Air Board tried operating the twin-engine Felixstowe F.3 and Curtiss H-16 briefly right after the war and quickly found them too large and unwieldy. What the Board needed was a high-powered, single-engine flying boat, preferably one that was readily and cheaply available as war surplus. The HS-2L filled this requirement well, and so had almost a monopoly on Canadian bush flying, which constituted a large portion of Canadian aviation. This dominance lasted until the late 1920s, when the high-wing monoplanes with air-cooled

A "fire sale" of HS-2Ls advertised in September 1923. Aeromarine was going out of business and perhaps wanted to unload its fleet. A previous full-page ad in Aviation *on June 18, 1923, had offered prices from $500 and up. (U.S. Air Services, September, 1923)*

engines took over. Even then, it was not until 1932 that the last venerable HS-2Ls disappeared from Canadian skies – the last of the type to fly anywhere.

The known users of Curtiss HS-2Ls in the postwar years are listed alphabetically by countries known to have had them, then alphabetically by known operators in each country.

Argentina

The Aviación Naval Argentina received six HS-2Ls in 1922 – A1206, A1224, A1225, A1257, A1264, and A1281 – which were shipped from the NAF on May 8, and a further four in 1923 – A2073, A2152, A2248, and A2249 – which were shipped from Hampton Roads on June 26. Only eight Argentine serials (T-1 to T-8) were assigned so, presumably, two aircraft were used as spares.

The HS-2Ls were based at Puerto Belgrano, Buenos Aires, and made training flights, including fleet spotting, until 1928, when the surviving machines were retired. They are believed to have been finished in naval grey with horizontal rudder stripes (blue-white-blue, with a yellow sunburst centred in white stripe). The wings bore roundels with light-blue outer ring and centre, and white centre ring.

Bermuda

J.A. Sanscartier of Montreal bought Canadian HS-2L CF-AEA/A1145 and Canadian Vickers HS-3L G-CAFI/A1258 in October 1930 and exported them to Bermuda, where he intended to operate them locally. CF-AEA was then registered as VR-BAA, but the other machine was not registered there. No other information is known.

Brazil

Six HS-2Ls, A1841 to A1846, were shipped directly from the Curtiss Aeroplane & Motor Co. to Brazil on July 24, 1918, with the notation "Transferred to the Brazilian Govt.," indicating a gift. The machines were assigned serial numbers 10 through 15 and assembled at the Escola de Aviaçao Naval on Enxadas Island in the Bay of Guanabara. Two were written off in accidents in 1919. On July 5, 1922, some Army officers rebelled and took control of the Forte de Copacabana, a modern fortress with long-range guns, but the rebellion was quelled the next day. Two HS-2Ls bombed the fort during the uprising, but their bombs fell into the sea. By 1923 only one HS-2L, No. 13, survived, and it was retired at the end of the year.

British West Indies

In November 1929 Canadian Vickers HS-3L G-CANZ/A1152 was sold to A.R.C. Holland of Nassau, Bahamas, and exported there. The aircraft was reported lost at sea and struck from the register in February 1930.

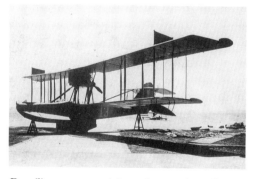

Brazilian HS-2L serial number 13. A small windshield was installed at the front cockpit to protect the observer. A Curtiss F flying boat, one of four obtained in 1918, is in the background. (SGDM)

It is also known that numbers of unregistered American HS-2Ls visited Bimini, West End, and other locations in the Bahamas during the 1920s to pick up cargoes of liquor.

Canada

Air Board

The Air Board was formed initially in 1919 to register and license aircraft, and license airports and aviation personnel as required by the International Convention on Air Navigation, which formed part of the Treaty of Versailles. When Great Britain decided to give a sizable number of aircraft to the British dominions, Canada formed the Civil Government Air Operations Branch under the control of the Air Board. As its title indicates, the branch would have no military function; its personnel would be civil servants, and almost all of them were ex-British air service personnel. However, a Canadian Air Force was soon formed to provide refresher training for World War I ex-pilots.

A variety of civil air operations were carried out, but the main ones were forestry protection operations, forest and land surveys,

The Air Board Air Station at Roberval, Quebec, in 1922. The larger and more permanent bases were fitted with launching rails. The three HS-2Ls are G-CYAE, G-CYAF and G-CYDY. The two on the left perform aerial surveys. The boxes on the right of their noses house air-operated intervalometers, which regulate the sequence of film exposures. The machines are finished in Air Board markings: naval grey throughout, with black registrations on white patches. (NAM 5090)

RCAF Curtiss HS-2L [G-CY]BB along the British Columbia coast. (CF)

fishery patrols along the coast, anti-smuggling operations, and transportation for government officials in northern areas. Air stations were established at Dartmouth, N.S., Ottawa, Ont., Victoria Beach, Man. (about 90 km [55 mi.] north of Winnipeg), and Jericho Beach, Vancouver, B.C. Substations were established elsewhere to enable

The Air Board Air Station at Jericho Beach, Vancouver, July 1921. A canvas Bessoneau hangar, typical of most Air Board air stations, is in the background. These hangars formed part of the Imperial Gift of aeronautical equipment to Canada in 1920. (NAM A17868)

HS-2L [G-CY]GA in RCAF markings at Jericho Beach in 1925. Wings and tail are yellow, the hull is white with red anti-fouling paint on the bottom; the roundels are red, white, and blue with blue outer rings; and the rudder has stripes with red leading. (CF)

operations over large areas and in most provinces. In addition subbases and mobile units were introduced to cover some areas when required.

The first Air Board HS-2L operations were carried out in the summer of 1920. The RCAF took over its operations in 1924, and the last RCAF HS-2L operations were in Vancouver in 1927. However, the last HS-2Ls were struck off strength by the RCAF only in 1928. The first Air Board HS-2Ls were ten of the twelve donated by the USN in Nova Scotia in 1918. Twelve surplus HS-2Ls were then bought in 1921 and 1922, one in 1924, and ten in 1925. Some of the originals donated were used as spares, and one of the last ten bought was not operated. The following 30 HS-2Ls were registered: G-CYAE/A1248; G-CYAF/A1875; G-CYAG/A1941; G-CYAH/A----; G-CYBA/A----; G-CYBB/A----; G-CYDR/A1991; G-CYDS/A1986; G-CYDT/A1990; G-CYDU/A1984; G-CYDX/A1993; G-CYDY/A1992; G-CYEA/A2019; G-CYEB/A1994; G-CYED/A1985; G-CYEF/A1988; G-CYEJ/A2223; G-CYEK/A2022; G-CYEL/A1987; G-CYGA/A1307; G-CYGL/A1298; G-CYGM/A1290; G-CYGN/A1312; G-CYGO/A1152; G-CYGP/A1159; G-CYGQ/A1303; G-CYGR/A1315; G-CYGS/A1392; G-CYGT/A1279; and G-CYGU/A1288.

This protective enclosure for the camera operator was devised by the Jericho Air Station. Known as the Jericho Beach nose, it was only fitted to HS-2L G-CYBB. The camera-hole has a visible protruding lens, a Canadian modification on many HS-2Ls. (CF106-VAN)

Bishop-Barker Aeroplanes' HS-2L at Toronto Island after its arrival from the United States before Canadian registration was applied. A helmeted W.G. Barker stands on the nose. (NAM 2034)

Bishop-Barker Aeroplanes Ltd.

World War I aces W.A. Bishop and W.G. Barker formed this company in 1920 to operate a general aviation business. The company also operated a short-lived air service between Toronto and the Muskoka Lakes district, a popular resort area about 180 km (110 mi.) north of Toronto. A single HS-2L, G-CADB/A1727, was purchased in July. The service operated mainly on weekends until a forced landing due to engine failure occurred on September 10. Pilot R.F. McRae and air engineer R.S. Baker were injured, but two passengers were unharmed. The aircraft was written off. A second aircraft, G-CADM/A1721, was purchased in October, but there is no record of its operations or subsequent history.

Canadian Aero Film Co. Ltd.

In July 1919, Blain Irish and Irwin Proctor formed this company to take motion pictures from the air. In 1920 the company got a contract from the Ontario government to conduct an aerial survey of the

Canadian Aero Film Co. Ltd.'s HS-2L at Moose Factory in August 1920, the first flight made to that northern area. It is the only aircraft to bear its Canadian registration along with its USN identification and serial number. (OBH)

Canadian Airways HS-2L G-CAFQ at Trois-Rivières in 1926. The man on the right is believed to be pilot F.V. (Turk) Robinson. (NAM 6292)

Canadian Airways air engineer/photographer Albert Simpson wing-walking on HS-2L G-CAGT in 1929, probably to show off his pure joie de vivre. (H.C.W. Smith)

area between Toronto and Moose Factory, Ontario, on James Bay. They bought a Curtiss HS-2L G-CAAZ/A2119 in July and pilot W.R. Maxwell made five round-trips from Remi Lake to Moose Factory between August 17 and September 12. On one trip Maxwell flew out a man suffering from mastoiditis. This was the first ambulance flight in northern Canada, and these trips were the first made into James Bay. The aircraft was destroyed in a barn fire the following year.

Canadian Airways (old)

This company constituted a reformation of Dominion Aerial Exploration Ltd. and inherited its equipment, including HS-2Ls G-CACS/A---- and G-CAEY/A----, in 1926. International Airways of Canada

Ltd. purchased control of Canadian Airways (old) in 1929; each continued to operate under its own name until both were absorbed into the new Canadian Airways Ltd. in 1930. Canadian Airways Ltd. operated from coast to coast, and from the American border to the Arctic.

G-CAFI and G-CANZ, two of the three Canadian Vickers HS-3Ls, commissioned and operated by Canadian Airways (old). (K.M. Molson)

Canadian Airways (old) continued to operate in the Lac Saint-Jean district of Quebec and along the north shore of the St. Lawrence River, carrying on the same type of operation as its predecessor. In 1928 it extended its operation into Ontario. It added seven HS-2Ls to its fleet between 1926 and 1928: G-CAFI/A1258; G-CAFP/A----; G-CAFQ/A----; G-CAGT/A----; G-CANZ/A1152; and G-CARL/A1288. The company also initiated the redesign and conversion of three HS-2Ls into HS-3Ls by Canadian Vickers Ltd. of Montreal, which was completed in 1928 and 1929. These were G-CAFI/A1258,* G-CANZ/A1152,* and G-CARO/A1143.

In addition to normal operations in northern Quebec and along the St. Lawrence, two special operations were undertaken. In May 1927 Charles Nungessor and François Coli had gone missing after leaving Paris on a transatlantic flight attempt. The company made two efforts to find the missing airmen in 1927. The first search originated from Trois-Rivières when pilot B.W. (Bill) Broach flew HS-2L G-CAEY to the Rivière aux Outardes. The next day he flew to Natashquan by 8:30 p.m. During May 16 to 20, poor weather and fog conditions prevented further flying. On the 21st, despite high seas, HS-2L G-CAEY took off, only to have engine failure soon after. Thus,

---

* The first two aircraft had been operated by Canadian Airways (old) prior to conversion.

the search had to be abandoned. Then F.V. (Turk) Robinson, in HS-2L G-CAFQ, took over the search along the St. Lawrence River and into Labrador from May 28 to June 4 without finding any trace of the missing men. The second operation was undertaken in the autumn. The company was commissioned to carry out ten experimental mail flights between Montreal and Rimouski, Quebec, to meet incoming and outgoing ocean liners, a distance of about 500 km (300 mi.). Company president Harold S. Quigley flew the first mission in HS-2L G-CAGT from Rimouski and brought 37 bags of mail from RMS *Empress of Australia,* saving 48 hours over the usual time. The following May, a regular mail service over the route was inaugurated with landplanes. The company's last HS-2L, G-CAGT, stopped operating in 1929, and the last HS-3L was sold that year. The company continued operating with more modern equipment.

Central Canada Air Lines' HS-2L G-CAFI at Kenora in August 1926. Pilot and manager W. M. Emery, standing on the bow, receives newspapers for delivery to area mines. (T.H. Cressy)

Central Canada Air Lines Ltd.

Formed at Kenora, Ontario, in May 1926, this company bought HS-2L G-CAFI/A1258 about six weeks later from Elliot-Fairchild Air Service in Hudson, Ontario. The aircraft had just been assembled but had not yet been used. J.M. Clarke of Winnipeg was the president and W.M. Emery was the pilot. James A. Richardson of Winnipeg took a controlling financial interest in the company. Then he became dissatisfied and withdrew his support. Operations ceased in October. The aircraft was later sold to Patricia Airways. However, this short-lived company gave Richardson his introduction to aviation and he went on to become known as the "Father of Canadian Aviation" in his support of Western Canada Airways and the new Canadian Airways.

Dominion Aerial Exploration Ltd.

Harold S. Quigley formed this company late in 1922 and took over the operation of the aviation department of Price Bros. Ltd., a pulp and paper company operating in the Lac Saint-Jean district of Quebec. Quigley had been chief pilot for Price Bros., and he started operations with his new company in 1923 with a single Martinsyde Type A Mk II seaplane. He added three Norman Thompson NT-2B flying boats in 1924 and three HS-2Ls (G-CACA/A----, G-CAEY/A---- and G-CAFY/A----) in 1925.

Dominion Aerial Exploration continued to operate the Air Board's former air station at Roberval, Quebec, and carried out forest survey and protection work in the area previously covered by the Air Board. In 1923 the Air Board loaned HS-2Ls G-CYAE, G-CYAG, and G-CYEJ to the company, and G-CYAG was written off in a flying accident with loss of its crew. The loan of the other machines continued into 1925 and 1926 and extended to successor companies in 1926.

In 1925, in addition to its forestry and survey work in the Lac Saint-Jean area, the company started exploration and transportation work for a survey along the north shore of the St. Lawrence River. In 1925 the company also took over the air station and plant facilities at Trois-Rivières, formerly operated by Laurentide Air Service. In 1926 the company was reorganized as Canadian Airways (old).

Elliot-Fairchild Air Service Ltd.

See Central Canada Air Lines Ltd.

International Airways of Canada Ltd.

This company was formed in Hamilton, Ontario, in January 1928. It first absorbed the Jack V. Elliot Air Service, which briefly retained its name. Then it absorbed Patricia Airways and Canadian Airways (old), the latter retaining its name. With Patricia Airways, International Airways acquired HS-2L G-CAFI, then being converted to a Canadian Vickers HS-3L. The resulting machine was registered to International Airways but flown by Canadian Airways (old). International also purchased an HS-2L that was registered to the company

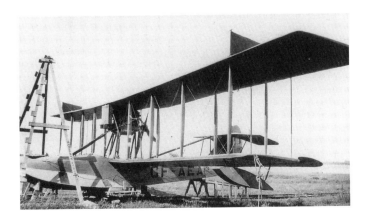

International Airways of Canada Ltd.'s HS-2L CF-AEA at Pointe-aux-Trembles, Montreal in 1929. (C.D. Long, National Archives of Canada)

La Premiere Patrouille Aérienne

C'est le devoir de tout citoyen
de nous aider a proteger nos
riches forets   -:-   -:-   -:-

First Aerial Forest Patrol

*IT IS THE DUTY OF EVERY
CITIZEN TO HELP PROTECT
OUR VALUABLE FORESTS.*

The St. Maurice Forest Protective Association Limited
THREE RIVERS, Que.

Chronicle Press.

A leaflet dropped during the first aerial forestry patrol by Stuart Graham in HS-2L A1876 for the ST. MFPA, June 1919. This was the first bush-flying operation in Canada and the first civil use of the HS-2L. (W. Kahre)

in 1929 as CF-AEA/A1145, the only HS-2L to be entered in the new CF-register. It was almost certainly operated by Canadian Airways (old) before being sold and exported to Bermuda in 1930.

International Airways and its subsidiary Canadian Airways (old) owned no HS-2Ls or Canadian Vickers HS-3Ls by November 1930; both companies were absorbed into the new Canadian Airways on November 25.

Laurentide Co./Laurentide Air Service Ltd.

The Laurentide Company, a pulp and paper company, became directly involved in aviation as a result of the action of the St. Maurice Forest Protective Association in 1919. This action was largely brought about by the interest of Ellwood Wilson, Laurentide's Chief Forester, in aviation as a new and productive tool of the paper industry. The St. Maurice Forest Protective Association was formed for the mutual benefit of a consortium of paper companies with timber limits lying in the valley of the St. Maurice River in Quebec. In 1919 the Association obtained the loan of two Curtiss HS-2Ls, A1876 and A1878, from the Air Board. Pilot Stuart Graham, ex-RNAS/RAF, was hired, along with air engineer Walter (Bill) Kahre.

Both HS-2Ls were flown from Halifax, Nova Scotia, to Lac à la Tortue in June – the first civil operation of an HS-2L, completed by June 23. Fire patrols, the first in Canada, were started about the end of June. The first fire reported from the air followed shortly after; by fall, experiments had shown aerial photographs could satisfactorily establish the type and value of timber from the air. Also, an exploratory flight had been made into the Lac Saint-Jean district.

At the end of the season some Association members withdrew their support. Laurentide was satisfied with the results, however, and continued its support for two years, but of course the work was confined to within Laurentide's timber limits. In 1920, in addition to forestry work, a company crew staked the first mining claim made with the use of an aircraft. It also further explored the use of aerial photos for forestry.

HS-2L A1876 launched at Dartmouth on June 2 or 3, 1919. Registered as G-CAAC in 1920, it was the first HS-2L operated for civil use anywhere and Stuart Graham chose it as the first aircraft for the ST. MFPA. Pictured here is Graham standing in the cockpit and Mrs. Graham seated in the bow cockpit. Now in Canada's National Aviation Museum G-CAAC/A1876 is the only surviving HS-2L in the world, and the subject of Part II. (W. Kahre/NAM 2703)

In 1921 new staff were hired to replace Graham and Kahre, who had resigned. W.R. Maxwell was hired as the pilot, and others as ground staff. Operations continued, but at year-end Laurentide, while satisfied with the results, decided that its aviation unit was too expensive to continue alone, though it would have liked the service itself to continue.

In 1922 a new company was formed, Laurentide Air Service Ltd., with new capital and officers. It bought three aircraft, an HS-2L, a Vickers Viking IV amphibian, and a Loening M23 Air Yacht. The staff was increased, work was obtained in Ontario, and a total of 688 hours of flying was logged. The new company lost its first two aircraft, the veterans G-CAAC/A1876 and G-CAAD/A1878, but both on takeoff, with no casualties.

In 1923 the company greatly increased its activities in Ontario; it added nine HS-2Ls and a Curtiss JN-4 (Can.) and expanded its staff. It also obtained a large building in Trois-Rivières, Quebec,

Laurentide Air Service HS-2L G-CADU only carried the company name on its anti-skid panels and bore no fleet number. Normally the company name was on the bow in various styles and in large letters. (K.M. Molson)

Laurentide Air Service HS-2L G-CACW, Fleet No. 4, 1923. That year, Laurentide was the first Canadian company to allocate fleet numbers to their aircraft. (R. Vachon)

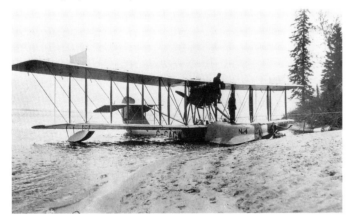

to house and service its growing fleet. Two machines were lost in accidents, the Loening and an HS-2L. In addition to its forestry operations in Quebec and Ontario, Laurentide Air Service handled transportation for a survey along the north shore of the St. Lawrence and into the unmapped area north along the Manicouagan River. The company carried out 1480 hours of flying in 1923, a sizable increase over 1922.

In late 1923 the Ontario government decided to establish its own air service, the OPAS. This had a serious effect on Laurentide Air Service. However, Laurentide did receive a contract to supply the new OPAS with 13 HS-2Ls, complete with modifications for Canadian civil use. This was done at their Trois-Rivières plant and deliveries started on April 21, 1924.

In the spring of 1924 Laurentide was asked by mining interests to start an air service to the Quebec Goldfields, the site of rich gold and copper strikes that consisted of a few log cabins in the bush and the beginnings of a mine. Communication was by water, requiring four different boats and several portages; it took approximately two days. The Goldfields developed into the twin cities of Rouyn and Noranda. A base to connect with the rail service at Angliers, Quebec, was made and a regular tri-weekly air service to the Goldfields was established. This was the first regular Canadian air service and it began on May 23. On July 31 the main operating base was changed to Haileybury, Ontario, to give better operating conditions.

Mail was carried from the beginning without charge, but on August 9 the Post Office gave permission to Laurentide to issue its

A 1924 Laurentide air mail stamp, fifth issue. Issues differed in minor details: one to three were green, four and five were red. These stamps were the first issued by a private company in Canada. (K.M. Molson)

Mining engineer and Canada's first scheduled air passenger W.J. Hacker (centre) stands on the dock at Angliers, Quebec, May 23, 1924 with Laurentide personnel (left to right) pilot R.S. Grandy, pilot and Director of Sales J.S. Williams, and C.S. (Jack) Caldwell, pilot of the flight. (T.M. Hall)

own air mail stamps. Stamps were prepared, and on September 11 the first regular Canadian air mail service began operation between Haileybury and the Goldfields. The service was an operational success but not a financial one. The problem was the usual bush flying complaint – the traffic was predominantly one-way.

In addition to the Goldfields operations the company carried out a number of other operations in Quebec and Ontario, and altogether flew 933 hours, carried 1 004 passengers, 35 034 kg (77,235 lbs) of freight and 554 kg (1,221 lbs) of mail. In 1924 the company issued an operating manual defining procedures to be followed, the first such manual to be issued in Canada.

In January 1925 Laurentide started a winter mail service to the Goldfields with a ski-equipped D.H.9C. However, the service terminated after only three days when the aircraft crashed without injury to the pilot. Following this incident Laurentide ceased operation. One HS-2L, G-CACT, was sold to Northern Air Services, and the other surviving HS-2Ls were sold as spares or scrapped. In its brief history the company and its predecessors established a number of Canadian aviation firsts and a secure place in Canada's aviation history. A reference to a more detailed account of its history is given in the bibliography.

The 11 HS-2Ls operated by the Company were G-CAAC/A1876, G-CAAD/A1878, G-CACT/A2260, G-CACU/A2267, G-CACV/A2266, G-CACW/A2276, G-CACX/A2272, G-CACY/A2275, G-CACZ/A----, G-CADU/A2261, and G-CADY/A----.

Northern Air Services Ltd.

This company was formed early in 1925 by B.W. Broach, formerly a pilot with Laurentide. Its headquarters were at Haileybury, Ontario, and it operated the route between there and the Quebec Goldfields, formerly operated by Laurentide, and also carried mail over the route and issued its own air mail stamps. Its operations ceased in August, when its aircraft, HS-2L G-CACT/A2260, burned in a fire fol-

Air mail stamps issued by Northern Air Services Ltd. in 1925 were dark blue. (K.M. Molson)

Northern Air Services Ltd.'s HS-2L G-CACT. B.W. Broach, manager and pilot, is seated with his leg over the cockpit. (K.M. Molson)

lowing an engine backfire. It had flown 169 hours, carried 503 passengers, 10 240 kg (22,580 lbs) of freight, and 467 kg (1,030 lbs) of mail.

Ontario Paper Co.

In 1923 the Ontario Paper Co. bought Curtiss HS-2L G-CACS/A----
and hired B.W. Broach as its pilot. The company had acquired timber limits on the north shore of the St. Lawrence River, and it wanted
to explore and survey these limits since many of them had not been
mapped. The aircraft was based at Franquelin, Quebec, just east of
Baie-Comeau, and their timber limits were north of there. During
the year, 97 flights were made, totalling 144 hours of flying, including some for aerial photography. The following year the aircraft was
stored, and in 1925 it was sold to Dominion Aerial Exploration Ltd.

Ontario Provincial Air Service

In the spring of 1924 the OPAS, which was formed by the Ontario
government in 1923, started operations, taking over the aerial forest
protection work that had been carried out by the Air Board and Laurentide Air Service. Its main base was at Sault Ste. Marie (the Soo),
Ontario, where a large, substantial hangar was completed by the end
of the year. It was capable of housing the complete fleet of Curtiss
HS-2Ls with wings removed.

OPAS's purpose was to patrol Ontario north of the agricultural
area, from between the Quebec and Manitoba borders north to
approximately the 50th parallel. Bases were established within the
area, and they varied slightly in location each year to suit the work
program being carried out. Aircraft would be sent out to the bases
each year about May 1, and they would return about November 1,
just before freeze-up. The number of bases used varied, but there
were usually between ten and twelve, and one or more machines
would be assigned to each. Obviously, in the event of a serious fire in
one area, machines would be moved around temporarily to deal with
it.

One interesting job in 1926 lay quite outside the usual fire protection work. In the summer of 1926 a rich gold strike was made in
the Red Lake area of Ontario. Men and supplies were urgently
needed before freeze-up. Ground transport could not do the job,
and at that time no bush flying companies were operating. Somehow
it was agreed that OPAS would step in. Three HS-2Ls were assigned to
the job in October, and work was completed by October 25. This is
the only known non-forestry work carried out by OPAS other than the
occasional ambulance flight for the injured or the ill.

Fire patrol and other forestry operations including survey,
transportation, etc., were done almost entirely by HS-2Ls until 1927.
The original batch of 13 machines was later augmented by others,
and a total of 21 HS-2Ls were finally included in the fleet. This made
the OPAS fleet the largest known HS-2L civil fleet. The only possible
larger fleet would have been that of Aeromarine Airways, but lack of
American records prevents determination of its final fleet-size. Some

*OPAS HS-2L G-CAOG being refuelled while docked.
A crewman adjusts the tailplane while standing in a
canoe. (E.J. Cooper)*

15 HS-2Ls were used by OPAS in 1926, the most ever; the number in use gradually diminished until 1932, when four were in use, the last HS-2Ls to fly anywhere. One, G-CAPF, was written off after suffering hull damage; the other three – G-CAOA, G-CAOK, and G-CAPQ – were retired in November. G-CAOA logged the highest air time of any HS-2L, 2251 hours in its nine years of operation. Beginning in 1927, when the number of OPAS HS-2Ls began to decline, they were augmented by other types.

Four OPAS HS-2Ls, G-CAOR, G-CAOE, G-CAOH, and G-CAOQ, ready for launching in spring 1925 after a winter overhaul at the Sault Ste. Marie base. (G.R. Hutt)

The following 21 HS-2Ls were in use by OPAS: G-CAOA/A----; G-CAOB/A----; G-CAOC/A2027; G-CAOD/A----; G-CAOE/A2014; G-CAOF/A----; G-CAOG/A----; G-CAOH/A----;★ G-CAOH/A2109;★ G-CAOI/A2015; G-CAOJ/A----; G-CAOK/A----; G-CAOL/A2070; G-CAOM/A----; G-CAON/A1367; G-CAOP/A1143; G-CAOQ/A----; G-CAOR/A----; G-CAOS/A1250; G-CAPE/A1300; and G-CAPF/A1342.

★ Two aircraft were assigned registration G-CAOH.

Pacific Airways Ltd.

Donald R. MacLaren, a noted World War I fighter pilot, formed this company in early 1925. The company bought a Curtiss HS-2L, G-CAFH/A1274, took over the west coast fishery patrol from the Air Board and operated a general air service out of Vancouver, British Columbia. In 1928 Western Canada Airways Ltd. bought the company and absorbed its aircraft and personnel. This firm should not be confused with the Pacific Airways Co. of Seattle, Washington.

Pacific Airways HS-2L G-CAFH at its Vancouver base. Its front cockpit has been considerably enlarged from the usual size. (C. G. Ballentine)

Patricia Airways Ltd.

This company started operations from Sioux Lookout, Ontario, in 1928 and had developed from an earlier company, Patricia Airways & Exploration Ltd., which operated from the same place but with headquarters in Toronto. It operated a single Curtiss HS-2L, G-CAFI/A1258, bought from Central Canada Airlines, and two other machines to service mining operations in the area. A year later Canadian Airways (old) bought the company and absorbed its aircraft and personnel.

Royal Canadian Air Force

See Air Board.

St. Maurice Forest Protective Association

See Laurentide Co.

Western Canada Airways Ltd.

This company was formed at Winnipeg, Manitoba, in late 1926 and commenced operations in the Red Lake area of Ontario. It expanded its operation quickly westward and in 1928 bought Pacific Airways of Vancouver. With this acquisition the company received its only Curtiss HS-2L, G-CAFH/A1274, which was used as a backup machine for the more modern types employed on fishery patrol until it was scrapped in 1929. The company later expanded into the new Canadian Airways Ltd. that operated coast to coast and from the American border to the Arctic.

China

The first indication that Curtiss HS-2Ls might be used in China appeared in the American aviation press in February 1920. A $500 000 consignment of aviation material was reportedly taken to China by the steamer *Dacre Castle* for a Capt. C.E.W. Ricou, formerly of the French Aviation Militaire. The shipment consisted of five Curtiss H-16s, two Curtiss HS-2L flying boats, two Aeromarine 39s, and two Boeing C float seaplanes, spares for the aircraft, ten spare engines, and various supplies like dope, fabric, etc. According to *Aviation*, February 1, 1920, the aircraft would be operated as "merchandise and passenger carriers along the Chinese coast and between China and the Philippines." There is no evidence that these operations ever took place.

All indications show that the shipment ended up with the South China Air Service (SCAS) that was then being created by Dr Sun Yat-Sen in hopes of establishing democracy in China. Dr Sun had already established a flight-training school in 1919 at Saskatoon, Saskatchewan. Later in 1922 he recruited Mr. Young from California, a Chinese-American who later became General Young Sen-Yat and, according to Dan-San Abbott, was recognized as "father of the South China Air Service." In addition, Dr Sun recruited an American, Harry W. Abbott, who was soon commissioned a captain in the SCAS. The SCAS used Curtiss JN-4Ds, JN-4Hs, N-9s, and HS-2Ls, but no details of their service are known.

In 1924 Abbott left the SCAS at the end of his contract and started the Abbott School of Aviation in Hong Kong. Abbott went to the Philippines and inspected and bought two HS-2Ls that were on sale from the United States Army Air Service (USAAS). They were used for instruction by the Abbott School. The school was sold in 1925 to a Dutch national, and Abbott returned to the United States.★

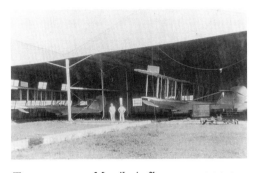

Two HS-2Ls at Manila in January, 1925, purchased from the USAAS by Harry Abbott (right) with Reginald Earnshaw, ex-mechanic RAF. (Dan-San Abbott)

Peru

There is little information on early aviation in Peru. However records indicate that the Servicio Aéreo Armada de Perú acquired at least six HS-2Ls in 1920, that their serial numbers were 115 to 120, and that they were based at Anco Air Station at Lima. These HS-2Ls are not recorded in the USN HS-2L record cards. While they might have been obtained through private American dealers, most countries dealt directly through American government agencies, and sales or transfers to foreign governments were recorded. It is also known that Peru operated Curtiss Seagulls during this period. It is

★ For interesting background information on Dr Sun and the flying school for South China students, see bibliography, Ray Crone, *The Unknown Air Force*. See also Dan-San Abbott's letter "Chinese Connection" and article "Rosamonde" for more SCAS information. For North China's early, but little-known, history, see Major De Senn Chung's article "Aviation in China."

possible that the report of HS-2Ls in Peru might have originated from confusion with the Seagulls.

Philippines

The USAAS was the largest operator of Curtiss HS-2Ls in the Philippines. They had the USN ship 30 HS-2Ls to Manila from March to August 1919. These machines were apparently all assigned to the 2nd Aero Squadron on Corregidor, an island at the entrance to Manila Bay.

While the duties of the HS-2Ls are not specifically known, it seems logical that the USAAS would make good use of the fact that HS-2Ls could land on any sheltered water of adequate size without the use of a prepared airfield. Consequently, the HS-2Ls may have been used extensively in survey work and communication duties throughout the Philippines. It is not known how long the HS-2Ls served the USAAS there, but two machines were sold to China in 1925, probably near the end of their careers.

In July 1920 the U.S. government approved the establishment of the Philippine Air Service (PAS) to operate an air mail and passenger service between Manila and other centres like Cebu, Iloilo, and Zamboanga. Two F-5Ls and three HS-2Ls were purchased, along with four spare Liberty engines and spare parts. The first HS-2L arrived and was assembled at Camp Claudio; Philippine pilots were flying it by the end of 1920. The first F-5L was ready for its test flight on June 3, 1921. Philippine officials were taken for flights, but their enthusiasm for the new air service did not go so far as funding it. In addition, when a new governor-general, Leonard Wood, was appointed, he ordered the abolition of the PAS. PAS equipment was handed over to the USAAS. The Philippine Air Service should not be confused with the similarly named Philippine Airways Service, Inc., which was also in existence at the time.

Portugal

Soon after the end of World War I the United States gave Portugal four of the ten Curtiss HS-1Ls and HS-2Ls stationed with the First Marine Aeronautic Company at Ponta Delgada in the Azores. The USN base was assigned to Portugal along with the aircraft. All the aircraft had been built as HS-1Ls, but some had probably been converted to HS-2L standards. The four donated aircraft, the A1122, A1126, A1130, and A1362 were still in their shipping crates. HS-2L conversion kits were included and, it is believed, a liberal number of spare parts. The U.S. records do not give the date of the gift, an unusual omission.

The crated machines remained at Ponta Delgada, stored outside until late 1922 or early 1923 when they were shipped to the

Portuguese HS-2L serial number 21 at Bom Sucesso, Lisbon. (FAP)

Centro de Aviaçao naval de Lisboa (Lisbon Naval Aviation Centre) at Bom Sucesso. Apparently, they arrived in poor condition. Only two were flown in 1923. The four machines were assigned Portuguese serial numbers 21 to 24. They remained at Bom Sucesso throughout their active life and were used for training purposes. *Jane's All the World's Aircraft* of 1926 reports that five were at Bom Sucesso then, which would indicate that another machine had been assembled from spare parts. The following year only two were reported there, and they were at the end of their service.

The Portuguese HS-2Ls were finished in naval grey all over, except for varnished wood interplane struts. The wings bore a large red "Cross of Redemption" near the tips. The rudder had a green vertical stripe leading and a red stripe trailing, and its centre bore the Portuguese arms. The serial number was carried in large black numerals on each side of the hull just forward of the wing.

United States of America

The United States began to control civil aviation only in January 1927 so there is no formal record of the number of aircraft in civil use or their owners prior to that time. In 1927 the HS-2L was at the end of its career, and only 11 are known to have been registered for civil use in the United States. However, the USN aircraft record cards list in some cases (but by no means all) the purchaser's name and date of sale of individual machines. These are listed in the company profiles below. It is believed that many more HS-2Ls were operated for civil use in the United States than are indicated. It is also believed that a good many of these were operated by rumrunners along the east coast. Unfortunately, only a very few records of this interesting, but illegal, activity are known.

An American civil HS-2L with passengers. This machine, converted from an HS-1L, does not have the standard American oil tank installation and still carries USN rudder stripes. (R. Liebermann)

The Pelican *taking off at Christmas Cove, Maine. Little is known of its operator, Travel Inc. of New York. Its controls have been moved forward and it seems to have a communal cockpit for six. (R. Liebermann)*

Aero Ltd.

Formed on July 26, 1919, with offices in New York City, this company operated Aeromarine 50 flying boats between there and Atlantic City and provided sightseeing trips. In September at a sale of USN surplus equipment, Aero was the successful bidder for five Curtiss HS-2Ls. The company was listed as having 15 HS-2Ls in 1920. In January, Aero started operating a regular service between Miami, Florida, and Nassau and Bimini in the British West Indies. This was the first regularly scheduled air service to operate in North America since the war. It operated in the Caribbean in the winter season only, and in the summer, shifted operations north to the New York City area and to tourist areas of northern New York State. During the ten months, beginning in January 1920, the company carried 4 500 paying passengers without accident.

Operations continued in 1921; about April Aero acquired control of United Air Lines of America, but no information about United or its operations is available. Pilots for Aero Ltd. included George Cobb, George Gay, Harry Rogers, C.A. (Duke) Schiller and Sidney Schroeder. Duke Schiller became well known as a colourful Canadian bush pilot. In late 1921 Aeromarine Airways Inc. took over Aero Ltd. and absorbed most of its personnel.

Early Aero Ltd. HS-2L with two cockpits. Possibly three or four such conversions were made before switching to the more common three-cockpit type. C.A. (Duke) Schiller seated on the bow and S.A. (Al) Cheesman (far right) later became well-known Canadian pilots. (C.A. Schiller)

An Aero Ltd. HS-2L at Lake George, N.Y., summer 1920. The black-and-white anti-skid panels were a new innovation. (R. Liebermann)

Aero Ltd.'s aircraft were finished in naval grey throughout; "Aero Ltd." was carried on the bow in white, and "Miami, Fla.," was carried aft of the wing on the hull. The anti-skid panels were finished with a white and black stripe with white leading, probably beginning in mid-1920.

Aeromarine Airways Inc.

This company was a subsidiary of the aircraft and engine firm, Aeromarine Plane and Motor Corp. of Keyport, New Jersey. It became the largest and best-known American air transport company of the early 1920s and the only one at the time to fly multi-motor aircraft. The company was formed in late 1920 by the amalgamation of two earlier Aeromarine companies. The first of these was the Aeromarine Sightseeing & Navigation Co., with headquarters in New York City. It operated two Aeromarine 75s (a civil conversion of the Felixstowe F-5L, carrying 11 passengers) and two Aeromarine 50s (a three-place flying boat). It made trips to various resort areas and carried out sightseeing flights. Also, the Florida West Indies Airways Inc. had been formed in the summer of 1920, but was soon experiencing financial difficulties. It merged with the Aeromarine company to form Aeromarine West Indies Airways. Soon afterward, the second part of the name was dropped, and it became Aeromarine Airways about May 1921. Late in that year it absorbed Aero Ltd.

An early Aeromarine Airways HS-2L coasts slowly toward dock in Florida. The company name, usually on the bow, appears in a light patch at the rear of the hull. The aircraft does not wear Aeromarine's distinctive black tail, nor does it have the company name on its non-skid panels. (A.O. Adams)

HS-2L Biltmore *preparing to hop passengers at Lake George, N.Y., in 1921 from the site used by Aero Ltd. in 1920. It is in Aeromarine's standard white colour scheme with black markings. (R. Liebermann)*

Aeromarine became best known for its F-5L operations on the Florida–British West Indies routes in winter and for its F-5L routes along the Great Lakes in summer.

Aeromarine's HS-2L operations received very little attention either in the aviation press of the time or in subsequent accounts of the company. On the surface this seems surprising: the company operated more HS-2Ls than F-5Ls, and logically, the HS-2Ls should rate at least equal attention. It appears the HS-2Ls were used partly as backups to the F-5Ls for over-capacity loads. However, they were also stationed at various points along the coasts and at resorts for joyriding operations and charters.

The Aeromarine Airways logo. (Aeromarine advertisement, source unknown)

It now seems that many, if not all, of these coastal activities were set up as fronts for illegal, but lucrative operations consisting of rum-running to a country gripped by prohibition. This being the case, it would not be surprising that little publicity was given to these HS-2L operations. Two accounts of these operations are found in Chapter 5, and there seems little doubt that such operations were widespread within the company.

These operations were much more rewarding than hauling passengers, and there is little doubt they helped to keep the black ink flowing in Aeromarine's books. Nevertheless, in September 1923 the company failed and ceased operations. It is believed to have operated a total of 11 of the twin-engined F-5Ls, and 17 HS-2Ls in 1922 and 1923. It may have operated a greater total of HS-2Ls but this has not been documented. In any event, Aeromarine had the largest fleet of American civil HS-2Ls and may have exceeded the largest Canadian civil HS-2L fleet of the OPAS. It was also known as the largest civil flying boat operator in the world, probably correctly. Aeromarine made a practice of naming its aircraft, but some machines were renamed when it was expedient to do so. Aeromarine aircraft were finished originally all in white with black markings, but their tails were eventually finished in black and they became known as the "black-tailed fleet."

In January 1924, Barron G. Collier and associates attempted to revive the Aeromarine operations under the name of Aeromarine Airways Corporation of New Jersey. According to the meagre information available, they attempted only the operation of five of the twin-engine F-5Ls. This effort quickly petered out, if indeed it actually started.

A. Alexander

Records indicate that A. Alexander of Norfolk, Virginia, bought HS-2L A2060 in July 1923. No other information is known.

America Trans-Oceanic Co.

Formed in 1916, this company had its head office in New York City and its main base at Port Washington, New York. At that time it had the Curtiss Flying Cruiser, an enlarged civil development of the H-14. Dormant during the war, the company was reactivated in 1919. By 1920 it had established bases at Palm Beach and Miami, Florida, as well as Bimini and Nassau in the British West Indies, and had assembled a fleet of six varied aircraft. It reported carrying 4 000 passengers and flying an estimated 129 000 km (80,000 mi.). Its fleet in 1920 consisted of one Curtiss H-16, one Curtiss HS-2L, three Curtiss Seagulls, and one Curtiss F flying boat.

The Curtiss-Metropolitan Airplane Co., which operated from the same office, took over America Trans-Oceanic in 1921. (The

Curtiss subsidiary was likely set up for the takeover.) The new company, operated from Port Washington and Palm Beach only, reported carrying 5 000 passengers, and ceased operations at the end of the year. It had operated one Curtiss H-16, two Curtiss Seagulls, one Curtiss HS-2L, and one Curtiss F flying boat.

American Aircraft Inc.
This company in Baltimore, Maryland, operated a general aircraft business from Logan Field, Dundalk, Maryland, and bought HS-2L A2109 in July 1923, probably for resale.

American Airways
This company began operations in 1921 at College Point, Long Island, New York, with one Curtiss HS-2L, and carried 600 passengers and flew 6 400 km (4,000 mi.). In 1922 it operated four Curtiss HS-2Ls, one Aeromarine 40, and five Curtiss MF flying boats, and carried 75 passengers and flew 2 400 km (1,500 mi.). It apparently ceased operations during that year.

Atlantic Airways Inc.
Operations started in 1923 at Higham, Massachusetts, with two Curtiss HS-2Ls, one Curtiss MF, and one Aeromarine 40. The company was active in Massachusetts and south to Newport, Rhode Island, and New York City. It carried 1 701 passengers and 680 kg (1,500 lbs) of freight.

M.D. Bryant
M.D. Bryant of Traverse City, Michigan, bought HS-2L A2265 in August 1923. No other information is known.

A.K. Coley
A.K. Coley of Hampton Roads, Virginia, bought HS-2L A2106 in August 1923. No other information is known.

Curtiss-Metropolitan Airplane Co.
See America Trans-Oceanic Co.

Easter Airways Inc.
P. Ewing Easter operated a two-place flying boat at St. Augustine, Florida, during the winter of 1921 to 1922 and ordered and took delivery of a six-place open-cockpit Curtiss HS-2L from Aeromarine in the spring. After several trips to Baltimore, Maryland, he interested some Baltimore men in forming Easter Airways with the intention of operating between Baltimore and Norfolk, Virginia and other coastal points. Two more HS-2Ls were ordered, but there is no evidence that the company operated them, or even that the new machines were delivered. Easter was listed as president, Conway C. Cooke, vice-president, and C. Delano Ames, secretary.

Easter Airways' Lady Baltimore II in Florida. A spotlight is installed on the strut going diagonally up the engine mount. (R. Liebermann)

Named *Lady Baltimore II*, Easter's sole HS-2L was unusual and probably unique in that a spotlight was mounted on the engine-bracing strut. It was probably the only HS-2L to have a light fitted; a light would be of little use on regular HS-2L operations but not so in the rumrunning business.

Eastern Airways Co.

This company, of unknown address, bought HS-2L A2271 in July 1922. No further information is known.

Finger Lakes Air Service Inc.

M.W. Blasier, Mrs. E. Blasier, and G.H. Leonard of Auburn, New York, bought an HS-2L and formed this company in July 1920. The aircraft, named *Auburn*, was based at Island Park on Owasco Lake. It was first flown by pilot L.H. Todd on July 28. It carried a total of 235 passengers in the Finger Lakes area that year. Apparently the machine was in an accident or destroyed in storage during late 1920 or early 1921, since a newly purchased aircraft, named *Mayflower*, arrived in May. Claire W. Purdy was the first to fly it. It left on July 21 for a tour of the Thousand Islands area piloted by W. Roy Benedict, who was later succeeded by W.N. DeWald. Business was good and 450 passengers, both American and Canadian, were carried. After its return September 10, the company announced that the *Mayflower* would be going south to Miami, Florida, for the winter; however, these plans were soon cancelled. The following spring the company decided not to operate the aircraft because of the Depression. No further information is known.

J.T. Gasleen

J.T. Gasleen of Portsmouth, Virginia, bought HS-2L A1395 in September 1923. No other information is known.

Great Lakes Airways Co. Inc.

This company operated from Cleveland, Ohio, and carried 100 passengers during 1921 in its HS-2L cabin conversion, almost certainly the prototype of this version made by Aeromarine. It had plans to acquire three more HS-2Ls but operated only in 1921.

Richard E. Griesinger

R.E. Griesinger of Keyport, New Jersey, bought Curtiss HS-1L A1453 in March 1927 from J. Morgan Corbett. As indicated in the U.S. civil register, it was modified by Corbett and the Aeromarine Co. by "cutting two holes in the deck for two extra seats and installing Aeromarine High Lift wings." It was then noted as a 4POSB(?), no wing detail recorded. It was entered as 7060 on July 12, 1928, the only HS-1L in the register. It broke from its moorings on August 21, 1928; the hull was crushed and a wing was broken. Parts were burned.

Gulf Coast Air Line/New Orleans Air Line

The U.S. Post Office decided to start an air mail service in early 1923 between Pilottown and New Orleans, Louisiana. Pilottown was at the mouth of the Mississippi River, about 115 km (70 mi.) southeast of New Orleans by air or about 130 km (80 mi.) by water. It was where marine pilots were picked up or dropped off by shipping. While the distance was short, appreciable time could be saved by sending mail by air.

The mail contract was given to two partners, Merrill K. Riddick and E.K. Jaquith, who obtained three Curtiss N-9 floatplanes to carry out the job. Riddick made the initial flight on April 9, 1923. For unknown reasons the arrangement did not work out. Arthur E. Cambas took over the route in June and formed Gulf Coast Air Line, which soon became New Orleans Air Line and flew its first run on July 2. Gulf Coast Air Line made 85 round trips between New Orleans and Pilottown in its two HS-2Ls and two Curtiss MF flying boats between July 1 and November 30. The HS-2Ls were taken off the route in 1924, probably because the mail loads were not heavy enough to warrant their use. Gulf advertised HS-2Ls for sale in their crates beginning on June 16, 1924, in *Aviation*. The route however continued with MF boats and later with other machines. One Gulf HS-2L was A2016, which was bought in October 1923.

George Hall

George Hall of Buffalo, New York, bought HS-2L A2120 in October 1923.

James Halstead

James Halstead of New York City operated an HS-2L, a Curtiss MF, and a Curtiss JN-4 (Can.) from Staten Island in 1922 and reported carrying 500 passengers and covering 2 900 km (1,800 mi.). No further information is known.

J.W. Hubbard

J.W. Hubbard of Tillsburg, Pennsylvania, bought Curtiss HS-2L A6510 in September 1923.

Hudson Valley Air Lines

This company announced plans to start operations with two cabin HS-2Ls in the spring of 1921 between New York City and Albany. It opened offices in Albany but there is no record that it ever operated.

William A. Hughes

W.A. Hughes of Norfolk, Virginia, bought HS-2L A2069 in July 1923.

Maxim Air Service

This company operated from Winslow, Maine, about 32 km (20 mi.) northeast of Augusta, and had a Curtiss JN-4 (Can.), a Standard J-1, a Curtiss MF, and a Curtiss HS-2L. It operated in the state of Maine and carried 300 passengers in 1923. No further information is known.

Robert Moore

An unidentified Curtiss HS-2L flown by Robert Moore, who was possibly the owner, was forced down by engine failure during a storm while flying between Miami, Florida, and Bimini, Bahamas, on March 23, 1922. All five passengers died due to exposure, but Moore survived.

New Orleans Air Line

See Gulf Coast Air Line.

Ohio Valley Aero-Transport Co.

This company announced plans to operate an air service between Louisville, Kentucky, and Cincinnati, Ohio. One hundred Louisville business men subscribed to its stock, and it intended to have several HS-2L flying boats ready for operation no later than July 15, 1920. No other information is known, and it is thought that operations never started.

Pacific Airways Co.

This company was based in Seattle, Washington, and operated one seven-place Curtiss HS-2L, *Bluebird,* piloted by Anscel C. Eckmann in both British Columbia and Washington. A plan to operate in Alaska did not materialize. It reported carrying 575 passengers and 450 kg (1,000 lbs) of freight in 1922. Its HS-2L was the Boeing-built A4248, which was registered N-CACM in Canada. This firm should not be confused with Pacific Airways Ltd. of Vancouver, British Columbia.

Advertising leaflet for Pacific Airways Co. (J. Eckmann, B. Eckmann)

Pacific Airways Co.'s HS-2L N-CACM was the only American-owned HS-2L registered in Canada. It was one of the few seven-place HS-2Ls in use. Pilot Anscel Eckmann is on the left side of the rear cockpit. (J. Eckmann, B. Eckmann)

Pacific Marine Airways' second HS-2L. (Harry Gann)

Pacific Marine Airways

Catalina Island lies about 48 km (30 mi.) off the California coast and is a popular vacation spot. It was first served by air in the summer of 1919 by Syd Chaplin Air Line, but this arrangement lasted only about three months.

In the spring of 1922, Foster Curry established Pacific Marine Airways to reinstitute the service. The company ordered two Curtiss HS-2Ls, the Boeing-built A4237 and A4251, which were sent to the Douglas Co. in Los Angeles for modification for civil use according to Aeromarine drawings. A4237 was made into the six-place open-cockpit version, and A4251 was made into the six-place cabin version. Service began on June 4, 1922, with the open-cockpit version at first and shortly after with the cabin version. Two return trips were made daily between Los Angeles and Catalina Island.

Service continued until sometime in 1923, when it is believed both machines were rendered inoperable. In 1925 the company was reorganized by Ellard A. Bacon as Pacific Marine Airways Inc. and A.C. Brown was, apparently, its one and only pilot. The company continued operating until June 29, 1928, when it was bought by Western Air Express Inc. (WAE) of Los Angeles. WAE continued the service with HS-2Ls until the end of 1929, when the HS-2Ls were replaced by Loening C-2H amphibians. This passenger service from 1922 to 1929, with a brief lapse in 1923, was the longest-lasting scheduled passenger service in North America up to that time, and, of course, it was operated only by HS-2Ls. It is recorded that 1983 passengers were carried in 1925, 4200 in 1927.

Over the period, at least five HS-2Ls were used, the original two, A4237 and A4251, and three civil-registered machines: 652 (ex-A1373), 2420 and 5419. It is possible that one or two others may have been used in the period 1925 to 1926. The wings and tail surfaces of 652 are now incorporated in the only surviving HS-2L in the National Aviation Museum in Ottawa.

Pacific Marine Airways' first HS-2L, the Boeing-built A4237. (Peter M. Bowers)

Pacific Marine Airways' HS-2L 5419 at their mainland base at Wilmington. It was one of their three HS-2Ls to be registered for civil use. (Boardman C. Reed)

Shank-McMullen Aircraft Co.

This company, with headquarters in Huntington, West Virginia, operated in 1923. There is no record of further operations, but there may have been some. The company operated in Virginia, West Virginia, and Ohio. It had a fleet of the following machines: fifteen Curtiss JN-4Ds, five Standard J-1s, two Thomas-Morse S-4Cs, one Curtiss Oriole, one Curtiss MF flying boat, and three Curtiss HS-2L flying boats (ex-USN A1259, A1303 and A1393).

Triangle Airways Inc.

Paul A. Townsend and Jay Colvin of Triangle Motors Inc. owned this company. It was located in Michigan City, Indiana, and operated an HS-2L christened *Desoto* in 1922. Apparently used for charters and passenger hopping, the machine was flown by E.R. Benedict and was serviced by mechanic C.F. Engaton.

W.C. Tiedman

HS-2L A6509 was sold to W.C. Tiedman of Brooklyn, New York, in June 1923. No further information is known.

United States Airways Inc.

William H. Warburton of Alexandria Bay, New York, formed this company at Albany, New York, in late May 1921. He planned to start a service three times a week from New York City to the Thousand Islands with a Curtiss HS-2L. Additional aircraft were to be placed on other routes, but it is not known if it operated or for how long.

United States Army Air Service

The American military air service operated under the name U.S. Air Service from May 20, 1918, to June 4, 1920, and then became the U.S. Army Air Service until June 2, 1926; for simplicity, USAAS is used throughout this brief account.

Apparently the USAAS first became interested in using flying boats for certain operations in 1918. It did not actually order any then; four HS-1Ls were transferred by the USN to the USAAS in 1918. Three of these went to Christobal, in the Canal Zone, and one to Hawaii. However, the bulk of the HS-1Ls/HS-2Ls were transferred in 1919. In all, 82 of them were turned over to the USAAS, the last being sent in 1920.

The odd thing about the USAAS is that while several books have been written about the history of the U.S. air services and their aircraft, the Curtiss HS-1L/HS-2L is never mentioned, although it was operated in quantity. It was not for security reasons: the USAAS's name was displayed on the machines, and occasional mention of the USAAS's use of the HS-1L/HS-2L can be found in aviation periodicals. The former USN serial numbers were painted out but no USAAS serial numbers were allocated. However, the USAAS name was quite conspicuous on each side of the bow; some operating units, but not all, applied a unit identification number prominently on the hull aft of the wing.

All HS-1Ls and HS-2Ls were assigned by the USAAS to units operating outside the United States, usually on islands where their

A USAAS HS-2L of the 7th Aero Squadron, France Field, Canal Zone, 1919. With a cylindrical gravity fuel tank above the wing, it is most likely a converted HS-1L. (SDAM)

water-basing capability could be put to good use. The units based in these remote places were unusual: instead of being equipped with all single-purpose machines (fighters, bombers, etc.), they were issued with a variety of types that enabled them to deal with almost any circumstance. The flying boats were often used for communication purposes between units; records show that Maj. Walter W. Wynne made the first flight of a regular mail run across the Isthmus of Panama, from the Atlantic to the Pacific, in an HS-1L, probably about mid-December 1918. HS-1Ls were also commonly used for survey operations and were invaluable in these remote places.

A USAAS HS-2L, Luke Field 212, at Kauai, Hawaii May 8, 1920. (R.L. Cavanaugh)

These flying boats were shipped by the USN for the USAAS units in the following locations in the quantities shown: France Field, Canal Zone, 3; Christobal, Canal Zone, 3; Coco Solo, Canal Zone, 1; Haiti, West Indies, 6; Hawaii, 11; Manila, Philippines, 36; Middleton, Pennsylvania, (Army depot), 11; unknown Army destinations, 10.

The serial numbers of USN machines shipped were the following: France Field, C.Z., A2161, A2202, A2204; Christobal, C.Z., A1811–A1813; Coco Solo, C.Z., A1123; Haiti, W.I., A1964, A1965, A1968, A1974, A1977; Hawaii, A1816, A2125, A2128, A2129, A2131, A2133, A2134, A2144, A2146, A2153, A2170; Manila, Phil., A2154, A2156–A2159, A2162–A2166, A2168, A2169, A2172, A2175, A2177, A2178, A2180–A2199; Middleton, Pa. (Army depot), A2126, A2132, A2135–A2143; unknown Army destinations, A1121, A1135, A1142, A1143, A1145, A1162, A1182, A1183, A1190, A1191.

United States Coast Guard

The USCG was formed in January 1915 by merging two earlier services, the Revenue Cutter Service and the Life Saving Service. It was considered part of the military forces of the United States and placed under the jurisdiction of the Treasury Department.

In 1916 two young officers began advocating the formation of an aviation section, and they were sent to the USN Pensacola Naval Aeronautic Station in Florida for flight training. Another officer was sent to the Curtiss Aeroplane & Motor Co. for training in aeronautical engineering and manufacturing. All subsequent pilots were trained at Pensacola, and early pilots were taken into the USN to serve in World War I.

The first Coast Guard Air Station was opened on March 24, 1920, at the former World War I USN air station site at Morehead City, North Carolina, but it had to be closed in July 1922 for lack of funds. However, it appears some Coast Guard operations continued from USN air stations until 1925 when funds became available, new aircraft were obtained and stations were opened. It is believed USN practices were followed in marking and identification.

While no information is available on the effectiveness of the HS-2Ls in aiding the anti-smuggling forces, it seems logical that they would have been helpful in locating the liquor supply ships stationed off the American coast. That being the case, it would have made the task of intercepting vessels carrying liquor ashore easier.

The 11 HS-2Ls transferred to the USCG by the USN are listed year by year as follows: 1920 – A2032, A2262, A2264, A2269; 1921 – A2263; 1922 – A1109; 1923 – A1374; 1926 – A1170, A1240, A1474, A1735.

United States Marine Corps Aviation

Several Marine Corps members learned to fly along with USN personnel in the early days of aviation, and the first of the USN members began their flight instruction in 1911. A Marine Corps flying camp was set up at the Philadelphia Navy Yard shortly afterward. When a permanent Navy Flying Corps was established in August 1916, it included both officers and enlisted men from the Marine Corps.

The Marine Corps came under the control of the Navy Department but was not part of the USN. The Marine Corps aircraft were identical to those of the USN and had the same serial numbers and colour schemes. After the mid-1920s, machines of the two services could be identified by "U.S. Navy" or "U.S. Marines" prominently displayed on their fuselages or hulls. However the USN record cards do not indicate the transfer of machines to or from the Marine Corps. Adding to the difficulty of distinguishing the two services is that they sometimes used the same base.

The first Marine unit was the First Marine Aeronautic Company, which was formed in 1917 and served in the Azores, initially equipped with Curtiss R-6s and later with Curtiss HS-1Ls and HS-2Ls. This is the only Marine use of HS-1L and HS-2L aircraft during World

War I. Inevitably, with the Armistice, Marine activities shrank, and by September 1919, there were only five active squadrons at four bases. The only post-World War I use of HS-1L/HS-2L aircraft by the Marine Corps took place on the islands of Haiti and Guam. The one unit with HS–1L/HS-2L machines was based at Port-au-Prince, Haiti. Six HS-1Ls/HS-2Ls were shipped there in 1919 (A1466–A1468, A1472, A1476, and A1477) and three more followed (A2124, A2125, and A2179) in 1920. The last two of these were stricken from the records in January 1922.

On Haiti, the Marine Corps was assigned to make a photographic survey of the entire island coastline. In addition, it operated a scheduled mail run from Port-au-Prince to Santo Domingo City, Dominican Republic, and to Santiago and San Pedro de Macoris, Dominican Republic.

In 1921 a new air station was formed on Guam in the Marianas Islands and a flight from the Marine squadron at Parris Island, South

USMC HS-2L A2026 overflies Guam harbour, circa 1922. The roundel on the hull, just forward of the serial number, is very rare and possibly unique on an HS-2L. (USMC)

Carolina, was assigned to the station. Some 16 HS-2Ls were shipped there (A1120, A1163, A1194, A1216, A2002, A2005, A2011, A2014, A2020, A2026, A4233, A4255, and A6553–A6556) and the last of these was stricken from the records in 1927.

United States Navy

Immediately following the Armistice many of the patrol stations on the east coast were closed, personnel were released, and equipment was dispersed to gathering points. The following stations were kept open with reduced personnel: Rockaway NAS, L.I., N.Y.; Anacostia NAS, Washington, D.C.; Miami, Fla.; Key West, Fla.; and Coco Solo, C.Z. In addition, Brooklyn Navy Yard briefly acted as a gathering point for surplus machines.

Rockaway NAS in the early postwar years was the base for large NC flying boats and continued to have HS-2Ls based there until the fall of 1920. It was closed shortly thereafter. Anacostia NAS continued to operate HS-2Ls until 1922 when the last one was stricken from its list. Hampton Roads continued to use HS-2Ls until the last one was scrapped in 1928. Until then, it used the type in good numbers since this was where Naval Reserve officers took their annual refresher training course on HS-2Ls – and Hampton Roads' HS-2Ls worked with the Atlantic Fleet based nearby. The Miami NAS continued to operate only on a small scale until it was closed in mid-1919. Key West NAS also operated only on a small scale until its closing in November 1919. Coco Solo NAS HS-2Ls continued to work with the surface navy in protecting the Panama Canal until the last of their HS-2Ls retired in 1927. During this time the tropical climate played havoc with the HS-2Ls' wood structure, and their mortality rate was high.

Dahlgren NAS was established in Virginia in September 1919 and was the only new NAS created on the east coast in the postwar period. It was 153 km (95 mi.) northwest of Hampton Roads and 64 km (40 mi.) south of Washington D.C. Its HS-2Ls lasted until 1928, and two of them were among the last three of the type to be stricken from USN records.

Moving away from the east coast, the Pensacola NAS continued in its role as the Navy's air training station. The HS-2L became its workhorse since its power and capacity made it suitable for a wide variety of training operations. Pensacola's HS-2Ls were usually USN leaders in accumulating flying hours for the type; the last four (A1117, A120, A1180, and A1238) were stricken from the Navy list in 1927. But it was A2016, retired in 1926, that set the USN record for flying hours with 964 flight hours recorded.

On the west coast, the San Diego NAS, which had only started in the fall of 1918, continued to grow until 55 HS-2Ls had served there

A USN HS-2L in March 1924. The upper-wing and anti-skid panels are finished in yellow. The aircraft is believed to be A2093 or A2095 from Pensacola NAS; the "49" is the air station identification. The exhaust stain on the left side of the tailplane is quite typical. (USNA)

– the last was stricken in 1926. Included in this number were nine attached to the Pacific Fleet based at San Diego.

Pearl Harbor NAS in Hawaii was established late in 1921. It operated HS-2Ls only for about a year when they were replaced by F-5Ls and other types.

The Guam NAS, in the Marianas Islands, was established in 1921 and used solely by the USMC. The climate at Guam, like that at Coco Solo, proved hard on the HS-2Ls, and the last four stationed there were stricken from the records in 1927.

It was in 1928 that the last three HS-2Ls were struck from the Navy list, two from Dahlgren NAS (A1140 and A1200) and one from Hampton Roads NAS (A1185). This does not mean the aircraft stopped flying at that time (they may have stopped earlier), but only that they were officially removed from the Navy list. The removal of the HS-2Ls from Navy service started when 31 were written off in 1926 and a further 19 in 1927.

The first HS-1L was shipped to the Navy in January 1918, and the last HS-2L was written off at Hampton Roads in October 1928. The type spent almost 11 years in Navy service. Every one of the 1218 built was carried on the USN records but many were not flown. Some of the unflown machines were scrapped in France, some were sold, some were transferred to other services, and some, unfortunately, just rotted in their shipping cases. Despite their 11 years' service in the USN, not all of these machines enjoyed long lives. In fact, like most wooden-hull flying boats, their actual time in service was probably short with a relatively small number of flying hours.

USN Curtiss HS-2Ls were finished in naval grey throughout. In the postwar years the upper wing and anti-skid panels of training and fleet aircraft were optionally finished in yellow to improve visibility in cases of forced landing. The wartime red, blue, and white roundel was optionally replaced by the star insignia in August 1919. The insignia became mandatory in January 1921, and the rudder stripes were reversed on its introduction.

Vermont Air Transport Co.

This company of Burlington, Vermont, bought HS-2L A2113 in May 1923 and A2027 the following September. No other information is known.

Western Air Express, Inc.

See Pacific Marine Airways.

C.H. Wissler

An HS-2L was sold to C.H. Wissler of Bellefountain, Ohio, in September 1923. No other information is known.

Gar Wood

Gar Wood of Detroit, Michigan, bought HS-2L A2004 in July 1923. Wood was a noted speedboat racer in the 1920s and 1930s, and A2004 was probably the only HS-2L to enter private use.

Chapter 5

THE AMERICAN RUMRUNNERS

In 1919 the Volstead Act, introduced by Congressman A.J. Volstead, was passed in the United States. It introduced prohibition throughout the country and was intended to prevent the manufacture and use of wine and spirits. In fact, large quantities were smuggled in, and further large quantities of very questionable quality were made and sold there. After strenuous efforts to stop the flow of illegal spirits, the U.S. government gave up trying to enforce the Act and it was repealed in 1934.

Most of the liquor was smuggled in by water by both Canadian and American vessels along the coasts and across the Great Lakes. However, an unknown but sizable portion of the liquor was brought in by land- and water-based aircraft. Few aircraft were caught, partly because of the medium in which they operated, but probably partly because American aircraft were not controlled in any way by the American government until 1927. This situation came about even though a convention on air navigation had been proposed. It was agreed to by all the countries including the United States as part of the Peace Treaty of 1919, which President Woodrow Wilson signed but the U.S. Congress did not ratify. This convention required all countries to identify and license their aircraft, and to license their pilots and ground crews. However, because the U.S. Congress would not pass the Peace Treaty, the air regulations were not put into effect in the United States. There was no way to identify an American aircraft or its owner until 1927, and by then few HS-2Ls were still flying. In 1926 the Air Commerce Act was signed by President Calvin Coolidge. It became effective in January 1927, and American civil aviation became controlled for the first time.

Most rumrunning operations were carried out by individual owners; while many operated water-based aircraft over the route to the West Indies, a few took the hazardous risk of operating landplanes.

Aeromarine Airways was the only known large operator to carry out smuggling operations. Aero Ltd. was the only other large operator along the east coast and there is no known evidence to indicate that it resorted to smuggling. But, of course, the temptation would have always been there. Many of the pilots were highly skilled; indeed, they had to be in order to survive flying by night with no facilities to help them. Consequently, when airlines started up in the late 1920s the smugglers easily found a more conventional piloting role with them. Pan American in its early days operated flying boats and quickly engaged Capt. Edwin Musick, formerly Aeromarine chief pilot and a smuggler, as their chief pilot. Naturally, he soon engaged a number of other skilled flying boat pilots, many with smuggling experience. Musick went on to pioneer the early transoceanic routes and was acclaimed the most respected and skilled of the early transoceanic pioneers.

Capt. Basil L. Rowe is the only one of the individual pilot-owners known to have written of his experiences. He did this in his biography *Under My Wings*. He located a damaged Curtiss Seagull, a smaller flying boat than the HS-2L, in New Jersey, repaired it, and headed south to Florida in early 1923. He related his first contact with illegal activity as follows:

> While hopping passengers at Miami another operator of a flying boat passed on to me a charter flight to Nassau to pick up a passenger. When I arrived in Nassau, I was dismayed at the size of the load my fare expected to get into one little flying boat. I was able to stow all of it aboard except one trunk. My passenger, a swarthy character from Chicago, told me that unless I carried all his stuff the deal was off.
>
> "The only reason I chartered your ship was to get this baggage to the States in a hurry."
>
> Finally I lashed the trunk to the motor struts atop the deck. I wasn't too certain I could get off with so big a load, and even if I did the wind resistance of the trunk might pull us back to a critical speed.
>
> "We won't bother about customs inspection," my fare said when we were ready to take off. "A boat's going to pick me up at the other end of the bay."
>
> I had cleared through the customs upon departure and I wasn't having any of this. "Well, you just cable that boat to come over here and pick you up. If you go with me you're going through customs."
>
> "O.K., O.K., O.K." My passenger apparently decided that whatever he was carrying wasn't too incriminating.
>
> Fortunately, we had a good easterly wind directly down the channel. It lifted the overloaded ship out of the water after a long run but the air eddying around the trunk set up a bad vibration throughout the structure. The drag of the baggage tied on the wing, plus the slow speed and the excess of power required, combined to keep the radiator close to boiling during the entire flight. On top of all this I began to worry about my passenger. There was nothing in the world to prevent him from poking a gun in my back and making me land at the place which he had originally designated.

What a relief when I put my keel down on the protected waters of Biscayne Bay in Miami! I landed downwind directly toward the door of the customhouse. When the officer inspected the baggage, I became more and more amazed at the contents, as well as at the brazen, self-assured manner of my passenger.

"What do you intend to do with all these corks and labels?" the inspector asked him. The labels were for Felipe II Brandy, Hennessy Three Star, ...

"My firm manufactures choice imported liqueurs," my passenger said casually, closing up his bags. "We have to have original caps and labels for the bottles – no counterfeits."

The inspector glanced at me and snorted with disgust. "That's what prohibition does for the country." He jerked his head toward my passenger. "He bottles all his choice liqueurs from the same barrel of rotgut."

My thoughts went back to my barnstorming friend who had passed on the charter to me. It was my first contact with something that played a big part in Florida barnstorming during prohibition years – rumrunning, as it was called.... Whether or not moralists approve, it was a very important link in the development of aviation.... Many a top air-line pilot learned his skill on the other side of the law. Only a few years ago one of our major air lines [Pan Am] established a base in Miami. The nucleus of the flying personnel was a who's-who roster of the famous booze brigade of the early twenties....

West End, Gun Cay, Bimini and Cat Cay provided ideal conditions for the booze brigade. There were several large supply ships anchored around the Bahama Banks. These undersold the land stations one dollar per case. It doesn't sound much, but it mounted up fast when you were making several trips per day....

It was a nondescript group that attempted to forge the liquor funnel between the British side of the Gulf Stream and the American gullet. But the crews were orthodox compared with the equipment they used. Every kind of airplane was represented. Any old crate capable of hauling a few cases was a potential blockade-runner. Landplanes were almost as numerous as flying boats, despite the fact that it was exceedingly hazardous to fly single-engine landplanes continually over that stretch of open water. It's still a question how many boys went down in the Gulf Stream.

Aircraft were rated according to their capacity in cases of liquor. A Curtiss Seagull was known as a twelve-case ship. An H-boat [Curtiss HS-2L] was a twenty-five-case ship, providing fifteen of them were gin, which was put up in fifths and therefore lighter than the case of quarts. It was mighty difficult for an H-boat that had been anchored out [and therefore water soaked] to take off with twenty-five cases of liquor unless there was a stiff breeze to help the ship on the step.

One of the pilots attempted to take a heavy load off from an open sea against a long, heaving swell that was running with a nasty chop. The heavy pounding was too much for the wooden planking, which finally gave way when the speed approached the flying stage. Fortunately it was the last swell that also bounced him into the air, scattering the lumber in all directions ..., but with careful nursing of the controls he avoided settling back onto the water.... The whole wide blue ocean showed through the gaping hole.... The ship would have to be landed on the sheltered surface of Miami's Biscayne Bay. The pilot fervently hoped they could somehow dodge the prohibition agents. It didn't occur to him to jettison the contraband. It had been paid for, and he couldn't afford to lose the money any more than he could afford to go to jail. Finally he chose a very brazen plan. By landing the plane as close as possible to the causeway connecting Miami and Miami Beach he might be able to beach the boat before it sank and thus save the load.

He made a good landing, but he was too close to the beach. The boat was still on the step and doing thirty miles an hour when the ship hit the shore. It stopped high and dry on the causeway, its bow sticking out onto the highway that joins Miami with Miami Beach.

"Lash the engine covers over the load and beat it!" yelled the pilot as he cut the gas. "We can come back later."

They were just leaving when a prohibition agent's car pulled up. The agent came over to the plane.

"We know you're carrying liquor," he said, "but we don't have the evidence yet. But some of these days we'll get you. Take my advice and lay off." He inspected the badly damaged plane. "What happened?" he asked. "Motor conk out?"

"It sure did," the pilot lied blandly. "Just as we were taking off. We couldn't clear the causeway, so I pushed it back onto the water."

The agent, convinced that it had been a take-off rather than a landing and knowing nobody would be hauling liquor from Miami in the other direction, said, "Well, we won't have to worry about you carrying liquor in this old wreck for a while anyway." He walked back to his car and drove away, leaving the pilot and his crew with a full load of booze where they wanted it, almost on a highway.

Bert Hassell's autobiography, *Fish Hassell: A Viking with Wings* relates how he became involved in rumrunning with Aeromarine. Bert had been running liquor in from Canada to Lincoln, Nebraska, in a Standard J-1, and he contacted his friend Edwin Musick, chief pilot for Aeromarine. Musick was looking for a good boat-pilot who had experience in rumrunning, so Bert was quickly taken on. Bert comments:

Ostensibly we [Aeromarine] were a barnstorming operation, using the boats to haul passengers for short sightseeing rides along the New Jersey beaches. We worked off the beaches during the day. We always had some business and it seemed to work well as a front for our bootlegging.

At night we would jerk out the seats to make space that was ideal for the bottled goods. All of our bootlegging was done at night, and because the business of landing on the open seas at night was pretty tricky, Aeromarine and Musick wanted a good pilot for the job.

Upon receiving instructions we would fly out beyond the three-mile limit but usually eight or ten miles to be sure and spot our trawler. Once we found the right ship we would land about half a mile away.

Hassell then describes how a small boat would put off from the trawler, towing cases of liquor that were paid for in cash. Then came the tricky takeoff at sea and flying along the coast until they got the all-clear signal from one of the possible landing places. Hassell left the operation after a while and began running liquor into Chicago from London, Ontario, in his own Junkers JL-6.

Hassell does not implicate any other Aeromarine pilots in the operation, but Horace Brock, in his excellent book *Flying the Oceans,* does. Brock says:

Musick had been a rumrunner as had several of the other [Pan American] captains flying liquor in from the Bahamas and from the rum fleet which only had to stay three miles off shore in the early days of Prohibition. Warned in advance [Musick's mechanic with Aeromarine] Johnny Donohue would be waiting for Musick on the County Causeway at Miami. As Musick landed the flying boat and ran up on the causeway beach, a truck would materialize and, while the Coast Guard and other revenuers came tearing up in speed boats, Musick and Donohue would unload the cases into the truck. Minutes later, when the government men hit the beach, there would be no truck in sight, and a relaxed Donohue and Musick would greet them with a present of a few bottles and a request to "lend a hand to push the seaplane back into the water."

Information available on individual smuggler's aircraft is restricted to HS-2Ls convicted of, or suspected of, smuggling as recorded on their registration record cards after 1927 by the U.S. Department of Commerce, Aeronautics Branch. Additional records may possibly exist with the USCG or other enforcement-agency files. Known information on smugglers' HS-2Ls is listed numerically by their civil registration.

318

Re-registered as 3732.

1849 (ex-USN A1145)

Bought by Charles H. Verill, Washington, D.C., from the U.S. government. At Arlington Beach, Virginia, in summer, and in Florida in winter. Reported sold in April 1928. No evidence of smuggling but thought likely.

2060

Bought by Richmond Airways Inc., Staten Island, New York, from F.G. Ericson, Baltimore, Maryland, February 1925. Sold to Wm. Wincapaw, Tottenville, Staten Island, (agent) 1927 and resold to H. Hedlman and L.A. Tarr, New York City. Aircraft flown in 1928 to Florida and, as noted on its registration card, "seemed to be on mysterious mission, did not dock with other planes or have anything to do with them. Reported down off Georgia coast and three aboard almost starved before rescue and plane damaged." Later reported "junked." No conclusive evidence of smuggling noted.

2821 (likely ex-USN A2222)

Bought from M.F. Worrell, Norfolk, Virginia, by Thomas T. Tyndall, Albany, New York, April 1927. Summer, Saratoga Lake, New York; winter, Miami, Florida. Reported sold in 1928 to Thomas H. Fennell, Saratoga Springs, New York. Previous owner reported using airplane for transporting liquor. Present owner also in bootlegging business. Aircraft later sunk on Saratoga Lake.

2932 (ex-USN A2021)

Bought by Charles E. Haynes, Miami, Florida, from Richmond Airways Inc., Staten Island, New York, in November 1928. Haynes reported a smuggler. See also 2983.

2983

Bought by Charles E. Haynes, Miami, Florida, in October 1926, from E. Epstein, Southland Jobbing House (sic), Norfolk, Virginia. Application cancelled in 1927 "as owner now held under $200 bond by Customs authorities. He is a confirmed smuggler."

3387 (originally USN A1162 transferred to USAAS)

Bought by T.B. Ward, Hialeah, Florida, August 1927, from George F. Rosenfield. Seized by Customs Department while being flown by William B. Atwater in August 1928 with 27 cases of liquor on board. Stored, then destroyed by Florida hurricane in September 1928. See also 3732 and 6845.

3732 (ex-USN A1191)

First registered as 318 to Lillian Hase, Duluth, Minnesota, and sold in early 1927 to Wilbur A. Hammond, Minneapolis, Minnesota. Aircraft overhauled and repaired. Had seats for six, had carried eight average-size people easily but normally carried five. Passenger-carrying at amusement park, Excelsior, Minnesota. Sold October 1927 to Royce Chalmers/Chalmers Airlines Inc., Miami, Florida and re-registered 3732. As noted in the February 28, 1928 entry on the aircraft's registration card, "this plane is one of my prize bootlegs and doesn't haul passengers except when customs get rather hot which isn't often. Ha!" Sold to S.W. Davis, Miami, Florida. Letter from Inspector Wilson: "My information is this plane was purchased by Davis with a view to smuggling liquor from British Bahamas. It is kept at Bimini, flown by William B. Atwater (formerly a pilot with prohibition forces)." Aircraft destroyed by a hurricane at Bimini in September 1928.

> 6845 (ex-USN A1301, originally transferred to USAAS October 1923)

Bert Krueger, no address, stored it "for several years" and then sold it to Biscayne Flyers, Miami, Florida, June 1928. It was stolen on November 17, 1928, from Roslyn Beach, Hemstead Harbor, New York, by William B. Atwater (see 3387 and 3732). It was seized by the Treasury Department, U.S. Custom Service, and sold February 19, 1929 to Finley W. Williamson, Burlington, North Carolina, who sold it April 4 to Raymond W. Mussellwhite, Wilmington, North Carolina. Repairs to hull were made July 1930. In December 1932 the owner reported it as "dismantled and salvaged." The dismantling date is not known but likely late summer; it is thought that this was the last HS-2L to fly in the United States.

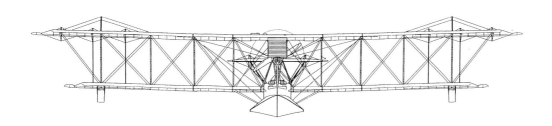

PART II

CURTISS HS-2L G-CAAC

LA VIGILANCE

A.J. Shortt

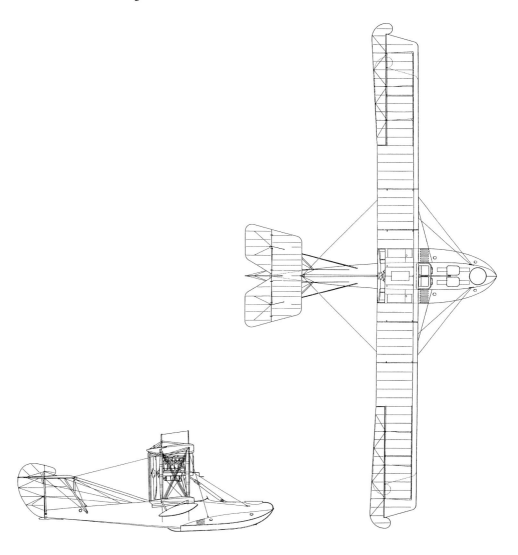

Chapter 6

THE HISTORY OF THE NATIONAL AVIATION MUSEUM'S HS-2L

USN A1876

The aircraft destined for fame and immortality as Canada's first commercial aircraft, the world's first bush aircraft and the only example of its type preserved for posterity, began its career with the USN in 1918 as the U.S. Naval Flying Corps A1876. Manufactured by Curtiss Aeroplane & Motor Co. Inc., with the hull subcontracted to Niagara Motor Boat Co. of North Tonawanda, New York, the flying boat was shipped to the USN on July 30. The USN had agreed to set up, equip and staff several air stations in Canada and to assist the Royal Canadian Navy in establishing an air service. As a result, the aircraft's connection with Canada began almost immediately when it was delivered to a new U.S. naval air station being set up at Baker Point, Dartmouth, Nova Scotia. Lt. (acting Lt. Commander) Richard E. Byrd, who gained fame as a polar aviator/explorer in the postwar years, was Commander of the station. From late September to the end of the war in November, A1876 and five sister HS-2Ls had logged a total of 184 hours flying from Dartmouth on convoy protection patrols.

La Vigilance

After the war the USN abandoned the stations set up in Canada and turned the Curtiss flying boats over to the Canadian government. As detailed in Chapter 4, Laurentide Co. Chief Forester Ellwood Wilson recognized the potential value of aircraft for forest survey and fire spotting. Two of the Curtiss HS-2L flying boats, A1876 and A1878, were obtained on loan and, on Wilson's recommendation, pilot Stuart Graham and engineer Walter (Bill) Kahre were hired by the St. Maurice Forest Protective Association. This event opened an important chapter in Canadian aviation history.

During June 5 to 9, 1919, Stuart Graham, Bill Kahre, and Graham's wife Marguerite (Madge) as the navigator, flew A1876 (now named *La Vigilance*) in several stages from Dartmouth to Lac à la Tortue, near Grand-Mère, Quebec. This flight marked the beginning of Canadian commercial flying and Madge Graham became the first woman in Canada to take part in a long-distance, cross-country flight. By June 23 both HS-2Ls were at Lac à la Tortue and Canada's first commercial air operation was successfully completed.

A1876 in USN markings with La Vigilance *painted on the hull bow and the ST. MFPA logo on the aft hull, at Lac à la Tortue, 1919. (CF/NAM 16926)*

Forest patrols commenced before the end of the month and bush flying became a reality. By the end of the season the two aircraft had proved effective in spotting forest fires and in determining forest composition and value (via aerial photography). Stuart Graham subsequently performed many other "firsts" during a very distinguished career in Canadian aviation. His accomplishments included

Crew members pull La Vigilance *from the water at Lac à la Tortue, July 26, 1919. Left to right: foreman /mechanic Walter (Bill) Kahre, handyman (Le Vieux) Cassette, pilot Stuart Graham, rigger Ernie Gouk, fitter Stanton. (S. Graham / NAM 11226)*

the design of the camera and camera-sight installation visible on the forward lower hull of G-CAAC, one of the first effective aerial survey photography systems.

G-CAAC

On June 2, 1920, *La Vigilance* was registered with the Canadian Air Board as G-CAAC, the third aircraft to appear on the Canadian Civil Register. During 1920 to 1922 Laurentide Co. and subsequently Laurentide Air Service Ltd. carried on and greatly increased in both volume and variety the work started by *La Vigilance* in 1919. Then on September 2, 1922, disaster struck the historic aircraft. On contract to the Ontario Provincial Government, pilot Donald C. Foss and air engineer C.S. Jack Caldwell were flying gasoline on board

G-CAAC freshly overhauled and painted at Lac à la Tortue, spring, 1922. (NAM 16437)

G-CAAC from Remi Lake to Lac Pierre to establish a fuel cache. On the return flight the weather closed in and G-CAAC was blanketed by a heavy downpour as it approached the Groundhog River north of Fauquier. With only sufficient fuel remaining for a relatively direct flight back to the base, Don Foss decided to land on a tiny, barely visible lake, rather than risk missing Remi Lake in the storm. Foss landed without incident and as he taxied slowly down the area of open water it appeared that a safe takeoff would be possible. The lake was a small north-south body of water with heavy brush growing right to the water's edge. To clear the surrounding trees successfully Foss realized that they would have to be airborne in about half the length of the lake, then begin a 180° turn to port before climbing

G-CAAC with sister ship G-CAAD at Laurentide base, Manouane, Quebec, 1921. (S. Graham/ NAM 14527)

above the tree level. Foss and Caldwell "lightened ship" by discarding non-essential items, then manœuvred G-CAAC until the tail was as far into the brush as possible at the south end of the lake. With Caldwell gripping a fallen tree branch to hold the aircraft in position for as long as possible, Foss started the engine and opened the throttle.

The takeoff began well. The flying boat lifted from the water and Foss commenced a gentle turn to port as planned. Deceived by the shape of the shoreline, Foss was forced to steepen the turn to clear the trees on a small point projecting into the lake. Foss looked

G-CAAC resting on the shallow bottom of Foss Lake a few days after the crash of September 2, 1922. Area residents reported that parts of the aircraft were visible above water for a number of years. (NAM 2249)

at the port lower wing to check clearance from the water and at that instant the tip struck the surface, causing the aircraft to cartwheel into the lake. Foss, knocked unconscious, was completely submerged in the cockpit, but fortunately Caldwell was thrown clear, onto the starboard lower wing. He pulled Foss out of the cockpit and soon they were both able to reach the shore. Well aware of their location, they set out to work their way through the dense bush to the Groundhog River. After reaching the river they met a trapper and his family, who helped them reach Fauquier. From there they travelled by train to Moonbeam Station.

A return trip two days later by canoe and on foot established that G-CAAC was a write-off. The hull was fractured in two places and there was extensive damage to the lower wings. G-CAAC was abandoned until winter freeze-up when a Laurentide crew returned to salvage the engine. It was removed and taken back to base but proved to be beyond repair and was scrapped. Undoubtedly, the first chapters in the story of this historic aircraft closed on a sad note.

Chapter 7

THE RECOVERY

G-CAAC Rediscovered

Over the next 45 years the remains of the historic flying boat deteriorated and gradually sank below the surface of the tiny lake. The aircraft's historic flights were recorded by the doyen of Canadian aviation historians, Frank Ellis, in his invaluable work, *Canada's Flying Heritage*, but G-CAAC had disappeared.

During the 1950s and 1960s a new interest in aviation history began to build around the world. In Canada a new awareness of the importance of aviation and aeronautical heritage led to the establishment of the National Aviation Museum,* the Canadian Aviation Historical Society as well as a number of other aviation-oriented museums and associations across the country. The general location of the G-CAAC crash site was known to a number of people. In fact, Dr K.A. Cheesman and OPAS pilot E. Culliton visited the lake in the early 1960s and made an unsuccessful attempt to locate the wreck by dragging with a snagging hook for several hours.

The subject of G-CAAC came up during a 1967 discussion among Kapuskasing businessman Don Campbell, Curator Ken Molson and Assistant Curator Bob Bradford, both of the Aviation and Space Division at the National Museum of Science and Technology (NMST) in Ottawa. Campbell was seeking information about the de Havilland Mosquito for an air cadet project when he mentioned that he had heard about an HS-2L crash site in the Groundhog River area. Expressing interest, Molson and Bradford asked to be kept informed of any definite information about the crash site. Campbell agreed, saying he would make a point of looking for the lost flying boat during flights over the area in his Piper Tri-Pacer.

True to his word, Campbell reported in September 1968 that he and his air cadet passengers had seen a submerged object resembling the shape of a flying boat in a small lake near Kapuskasing. Bob

---

* The National Aviation Museum opened at Uplands Airport in Ottawa in 1960. The aircraft collections of the National Aviation Museum, Canadian War Museum and the RCAF were consolidated at Rockcliffe Airport in 1964 and officially named the National Aeronautical Collection in 1965. NAM and the NAC became the Air and Space Division of the National Museum of Science and Technology in 1968. In anticipation of the new building then under construction, the Division reverted back to its original name, the National Aviation Museum, in 1982.

Foss Lake from the air, 1968. (Mac McIntyre/ NAM 18564)

Bradford was excited about the possibility of locating the remains of a Curtiss HS-2L. Even more exciting was the news that older local residents were sure that the crash site dated from before the establishment of the OPAS base at Remi Lake. The aircraft, therefore, could be G-CAAC! Dr D.M. Baird, NMST Director, was impressed by Bradford's enthusiasm and agreed that Bradford should visit the site to determine the identity of the remains and to decide if a recovery was possible. Arrangements were made for a few hours' use of a Dominion Helicopter Bell Jet Ranger, courtesy of the Ontario Department of Lands and Forests. On September 20, Bradford and Campbell were flown from Kapuskasing to the small lake.

As the helicopter flew low and slowly over the lake, the men saw the shape of the rear section of the flying boat hull, surrounded by what appeared to be pieces of silver fabric. Also apparent was the shape of wing spars extending out from the hull at an awkward angle and disappearing into the silt on the lake bottom. The pilot landed immediately over the wreckage, and a pulp hook was used to snag a visible piece of structure. A portion of the port stabilizer spar, a compression rib, and a hull-to-rib support strut were recovered. The configuration of these components appeared to be compatible with an HS-2L, making additional investigation worthwhile. The helicopter returned the party with their discoveries to Kapuskasing and plans were made for a more comprehensive survey of the crash site.

A de Havilland Canada Beaver was rented from White River Air Service at Bradley Bay on Remi Lake and Campbell borrowed grappling hooks from the local police. The Beaver pilot, Gary Thomson, had heard of the wrecked aircraft and quickly became an enthusiastic supporter. The party soon flew back to the lake, this time with a canoe. As the Beaver returned to Remi Lake, Bradford and Campbell began retrieving components from the silt-covered lake bottom.

The first major item raised was an almost-complete rudder with the distinct HS-2L shape confirming the aircraft type. Fragments of the silver fabric were collected, some of which showed evidence of the aircraft's registration in black lettering, including a considerable part of a large "G." As would be expected after 46 years in the lake, the aircraft was a tangled mass. Visible parts, principally the aft section of the hull were badly eroded, but fortunately, the lake's deep silt had remarkable preservative qualities. Components buried in the silt were in quite good condition. A comparison of the port and starboard metal rudder horns was a textbook example of the silt's preservative qualities. One horn, which had been covered by the silt, was in excellent condition, while the other horn, which had been exposed to water, had crumbled almost completely away. Over the next two years as the Museum crew members worked to recover the HS-2L they would curse the sticky, evil-smelling silt as it clouded the water and destroyed visibility or clung tenaciously to the crew's skin and clothes. Yet at the same time everyone was thankful that the silt had preserved major parts of Canada's first commercial aircraft.

Two days of grappling by Bradford and Campbell, assisted by Campbell's son Glenn on the second day, brought up numerous other small components and many pieces of the silver fabric. On closer examination, the fabric proved to be silver dope with only the impression of the original fabric left on the underside. Nevertheless these large flakes of dope were eventually very useful in establishing the size and configuration of the registration and other markings on the aircraft. However, the small group had found it impossible to recover any large components and the appearance of the badly deteriorated structure in 1 to 1.5 m deep water was less than encouraging. At this point, not one positive clue to the identity of the HS-2L had been uncovered. Had the aircraft been a less important type, the operation would have been abandoned.

The possibility of recovering major parts of an HS-2L, perhaps even G-CAAC, convinced Bradford to recommend more extensive underwater archaeology. Bill Swann of the Spruce Falls Pulp & Paper Co. arranged permission for the Museum crew to work on timber rights property. By the end of September two National Aeronautical Collection (NAC) staff members, Chief Restoration Officer Bill Merrikin and Technician Barry Mackeracher, had flown into the lake with more elaborate equipment to establish a campsite, complete with a small dock. Bradford returned and together with the crew commenced recovering components. An amazing collection of smaller items was recovered including many metal turnbuckles, pulleys, and fittings. Everything below the silt level was well preserved, raising expectations that really exciting buried treasures would be found. Probing in the silt confirmed these hopes when the crew discovered that a large part of the forward hull remained in solid condition.

Barry Mackeracher (left) and Bill Merrikin use two canoes to make a stable recovery platform. (R. W. Bradford/NAM 17046)

The weather by this time had deteriorated with rain and snow falling during most of the four days spent at the site. The crew decided to pack up for the season and make plans for a maximum effort in the summer of 1969. In the meantime, all wood components were preserved by applying Carbowax 1540, a polyethylene glycol material that had been used successfully in preserving the Swedish warship *Vaasa,* which was raised after 300 years under the sea. Application of the Carbowax was tricky at first, but once mastered, was relatively simple though messy. After more than 20 years it is still fully effective.

Although most documentary evidence confirmed the site as the place where G-CAAC had crashed on September 2, 1922, there was still no positive physical evidence. Over the winter Bradford contacted Stuart Graham, who had made the first bush flights 50 years before, and through Graham made contact with Don Foss, pilot on the last flight of G-CAAC. Correspondence and conversations with these two pioneers confirmed within reason that the HS-2L in question was in fact G-CAAC. Documentation provided by Graham confirmed that G-CAAC was the original *La Vigilance*. It now appeared certain that the operation begun in the hope of recovering components of an HS-2L had in fact located one of the most significant aircraft in Canada's aeronautical history.

G-CAAC Recovered

During the winter and spring of 1969 thorough plans and preparations were made for a major effort to begin in August. Equipment was purchased, rented or borrowed and most important, volunteer help from several organizations and individuals was secured. The Honourable René Brunelle of the Ontario Ministry of Natural Resources arranged the use, when available, of the Department's de Havilland Canada Turbo Beaver stationed at Remi Lake. The Canadian Armed Forces agreed to airlift the recovered components out of the camp by helicopter. Capt. Tom Calow of Canadian Forces Base North Bay offered his services and those of six other members of the North Bay Aquajets Scuba Diving Club, Terry Clark, Bob Braund, Dave Westell, Vic Yankee, Rick Bouffard, and Hal Rudovsky. The skilled assistance of these seven divers was critical in the recovery process. Don Campbell continued his invaluable assistance and Mac McIntyre, an old friend of the Museum, donated his time, bush salvage experience and unfailing good humour. Members of Kapuskasing 647 Air Cadet Wing also provided welcome assistance. The Department of Energy, Mines and Resources loaned two

Mac McIntyre holds lower section of rudder after recovery, August 1969. (R.W. Bradford/NAM 16944)

22 730-L (5,000-gallon) per hour gasoline-powered pumps, camping equipment and a VHF radio. Another pump was borrowed from the Department of Lands and Forests. Without all these generous offers as well as the help of many others, the success of the operation would not have been possible.

In early August, NAC staff, Bob Bradford, Chuck Aylen, Barry Mackeracher and summer student Maurice Madore, along with Bill Hiscock (on loan from NMST until August 8), assembled at Chalet Brunelle near the Department of Lands and Forests Base at Remi Lake. On August 6 the crew, flown by enthusiastic Lands and Forests pilot Don McLellan, began moving supplies and equipment to the lake and clearing a campsite. The next day the volunteer divers

Divers working from the raft over the recovery site, August 7, 1969. (R.W. Bradford/NAM 16941)

Painting by R.W. Bradford depicts divers clearing the 47-year build-up of silt that protected the lower hull. (NAM 13109)

arrived, the camp was established and a 4.88-metres-square (16-feet-square) raft was constructed from 4-ft × 8-ft sheets of 3/4-in. plywood, cedar poles and empty fuel drums. Two gasoline-powered pumps to vacuum silt were mounted, one on each end of the raft with 6-m (20-ft) intake pipes and 15-m (50-ft) exhaust pipes. By the end of the day, the divers had brought up several large components and had made tentative assessments of the surviving hull by probing with their hands through the silt. That evening and most following evenings Campbell flew over the lake for radio briefings on the operation's progress. Back on the ground at Kapuskasing he relayed messages and requests as necessary.

The next day, working at an exhausting pace, the divers discovered the entire lower hull intact. They were able to free the hull from

Aerial view of the camp at Foss Lake shows the 4.88-metres-square (16-feet-square) raft in place over the recovery site. (B.D. Mackeracher /NAM 16386)

The hard-working Ontario Ministry of Natural Resources' de Havilland Canada Turbo Beaver at the camp dock, August 1969. (W. Green, Northern Times /NAM 16958)

The Foss Lake camp as seen from the recovery raft. (B.D. Mackeracher /NAM 18628)

the silt and partially raise it in the water by lashing two water-filled fuel drums inside the hull and then pumping out the water to create buoyancy. Throughout the day they recovered many other interesting items including such major structural components as wing spars, ribs, empennage sections, an amazing collection of instruments and aircraft equipment, and a complete set of engine tools. This was not surprising. During the 1920s aircraft crews had to be prepared for any eventuality. Other items recovered even included a full-size blowtorch, a spare generator, an ignition kit, spare gears for the Liberty engine, a storage battery, a fire extinguisher, and many other

G-CAAC's stern is brought ashore. The inflated inner tube provided buoyancy and protection and the fuel drum was pumped dry underwater to help raise the hull. (R.W. Bradford/NAM 16931)

tools and components. One particularly welcome discovery was a segment of the cockpit area crudely painted with the letters AAC – the first physical evidence that this was the historic G-CAAC.

The crew spent the next day, August 9, recovering more components and tools and moving the still-submerged hull to shallow water near shore for closer examination. By gently towing the hull at a constant speed it could be moved through the water without dragging or bouncing too heavily on the lake bottom. That same day a journalist arrived from the Kapuskasing *Northern Times,* the first of many representatives from the news media to visit and report on the

Bob Bradford holds the first physical evidence that the HS-2L is G-CAAC. (NAM 15479)

Crew members move the forward hull section to shore with the fuel floatation drum secured with netting. (R.W. Bradford/NAM 16930)

Blowtorch, soldering equipment, and two funnels (nested together) found in the hull. (R.W. Bradford/NAM 16387)

Camera port plug, battery, generator, distributor cap, .303 cartridges, and other items recovered from the lake. (R.W. Bradford/NAM 16405)

operation. Mac McIntyre and two air cadet volunteers, Bernie Scott and Milt Atkins, also arrived to help in the recovery.

Sunday, August 10, was a landmark day for the operation. The hull was towed slowly, stern first, to a plywood slipway beside the camp dock. Barry Mackeracher, who had brought his bagpipes to the camp for just such an occasion, piped the historic aircraft ashore.

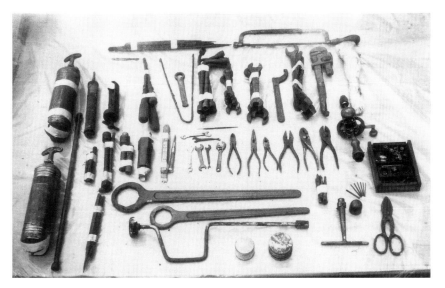

Fire extinguishers and tools, some found in the hull and others found in the silt below the hull. (R.W. Bradford/NAM 16385)

Final proof: remains of the registration letters "G-CAAC" on the starboard side of the aft hull. (R.W. Bradford/NAM 18314)

Chuck Aylen cleans silt from the inside of the aft hull section as Barry Mackeracher and Moe Madore discuss the operation and support the hull. (R.W. Bradford/NAM 16943)

As the hull emerged from the silt-clouded water the crew noticed that a section of rear starboard side-planking had been folded over by lashings for one of the fuel drums used for floatation. When the lashings were removed and the planking was restored to an upright position, cheers rang out. A major part of the registration letters G-CAAC was in amazingly good condition on the side of the hull, confirming the aircraft's identity. The surviving section of hull was in surprisingly sound condition and one pump was set up to provide a light spray of water over the entire structure. This helped the wood to adjust to a new environment and provided the crew with an unexpected bonus – the perfect shower for rinsing off silt. Their mission successful, the divers departed the next day, leaving the remainder of the crew to assess the recovered treasures.

The complete hull on shore at the campsite. (R.W. Bradford/NAM 16945)

The copper upper-centre section gravity-feed fuel tank. Like many other recovered G-CAAC components it is now installed in the reconstruction of G-CAAC. (R.W. Bradford/NAM 16399)

The recovered lower hull was reasonably solid and complete in spite of the crash, the subsequent years of exposure, and the unavoidable rigors of the recovery operation. There was damage in several areas to the upper surface mahogany planking of the port and starboard sponsons. The double planking of the hull bottom also had been holed in two places during the crash; one large smashed-out section on the port side under the cockpit area accounted for the

A section of the cockpit floor complete with the rudder bar and foot plates. (R.W. Bradford/NAM 16398)

Left to right: Moe Madore, Mac McIntyre, Barry Mackeracher, a volunteer air cadet, and Chuck Aylen hold up the port upper-front spar and leading edge, which are supported by attached interplane struts. The air cadet supports the aft anti-skid panel kingpost. (B.D. Mackeracher /NAM 18629)

numerous tools and other items found buried in the silt. Many other small items such as .303 rifle ammunition, needle files and other tools were found in the hull. Excitement and joy described the mood when the crew found the manufacturer's plate on the structural member behind the pilot and engineer seats. The plate, which was in fine condition, was marked: "BUILT BY NIAGARA MOTORBOAT COMPANY, NORTH TONAWANDA, N.Y. BUILDER'S NO. 2901-H.2 COMPLETED 7-9-18, WT. OF BARE HULL 975." This confirmed that the hull was manufactured by a Curtiss HS-2L subcontractor as noted in the *HS-2L Methods Manual* held by the Museum library. The hull and all other recovered components were preserved with a solution of Carbowax 1540 and water, applied either by brush or by

A control-wheel segment, engine throttle, and spark controls are immersed in a Carbowax 1540/water mixture for preservation. (R.W. Bradford /NAM 16394)

Left to right: Chuck Aylen, Mac McIntyre, Barry Mackeracher, and Moe Madore install plywood siding to the forward hull crate. (R.W. Bradford/ NAM 16401)

Moe, Chuck, and Barry lift the forward hull with a block and tackle suspended from an improvised tripod. (R.W. Bradford /NAM 16384)

immersion. Later in the Museum workshop at Rockcliffe, the hull and other large components were subjected to a fine spray of the same solution for several days to ensure thorough coverage and penetration. In subsequent years, the Carbowax has presented many "housekeeping" problems because of its tendency to liquify and drip in warm humid conditions. But its preservation qualities certainly outweigh this inconvenience.

With recovery from the lake bottom completed, the next task was to prepare the components for movement by helicopter from the lake to the Kapuskasing airport. The hull was cut into two manageable sections by severing the keel just aft of the sponsons. The aft hull

Illustration by R. W. Bradford shows the components of G-CAAC recovered from Foss Lake, 1968–69. (R. W. Bradford)

section was small enough to be easily crated and lifted by helicopter, but the large forward hull presented a more difficult problem. Bill Merrikin arrived for the final preparation stage and suggested that a large open-bottom crate be manufactured to cradle the hull during airlift and transport. The crate would be suspended on a sling beneath the helicopter, thus allowing the powerful down-wash from the helicopter rotor blades to pass through without excessive strain on the crate or the sling.

As preparations proceeded on shore, Mac McIntyre and two air cadets continued to search the lake bottom using a glass-bottom view box, drag hooks and a net. They recovered several more components and a quantity of large silver dope flakes, many with letters or partial letters of registration and other markings. These would later prove crucial in establishing the paint scheme for the aircraft. During this period the recovery operation became quite well known and a surprising number of interested people, news media representatives and government officials visited the camp. The Honourable John Robarts, Premier of Ontario, the Honourable René Brunelle, Minister of Natural Resources and the Honourable James Auld, Minister of Tourism were such visitors. Dr D.M. Baird also flew in to view and photograph the operation.

Despite the generally poor weather throughout late August and early September, the crew made excellent progress. They moved smaller components to Kapuskasing airport where Bob Laberge, Department of Transport Airport Manager, offered to store them until they could be transported to Ottawa. At the camp the two hull sections were carefully crated using 2-in × 6-in planks and 4-ft × 8-ft sheets of plywood. Trees were cut and brush was removed to clear a 61-m (200-ft) diameter area for a helicopter landing pad. By September 7 all was ready. The camp was dismantled and the equipment as well as smaller HS-2L components were flown out. After several flights the Turbo Beaver suffered a fuel-control problem and for a time it seemed that Bill Merrikin, Chuck Aylen and Barry Mackeracher would be stranded in the open overnight at the camp. Fortunately before nightfall Harry Dale flew a Dominion Helicopter Bell 47 into Kapuskasing airport and permission to use the helicopter was obtained. In two trips everyone was out and plans were made for the final airlift. A Canadian Armed Forces Piasecki H-21 helicopter of the Trenton 424 Transport and Rescue Squadron was in Sault Ste. Marie on a search mission. Assigned to lift the HS-2L hull sections out after completion of its mission, the H-21 arrived at Kapuskasing on Friday, September 12. Enthused about the airlift, Capt. Perry Cunningham and his crew, Capt. Gesner, Cpl. St. George and Cpl. Kennedy, immediately flew to the campsite with Bradford and several other team members to inspect the area. A small amount of additional clearing was required, then all was ready.

The next day, on the first flight, the Museum staff and two of the H-21 crew members were dropped off to attach cables and to prepare the hull crate for airlift. Remaining HS-2L components were brought out and the H-21 returned a second time for the aft hull. It

Preparing to load recovered components into the H-21, September 13, 1969. (B.D. Mackeracher/ NAM 16955)

was loaded into the helicopter's cabin with the stern protruding from the cargo door and was flown out without incident. The H-21 returned for the most difficult part of the operation. With the Turbo Beaver back in operation, Don McLellan and Guy Laroche took Bob Bradford and editor of *Northern Times* Wayne Green to Foss Lake to photograph the airlift. The big H-21 hovered over the recovery area. The external sling was hooked up to the HS-2L crate and liftoff proceeded successfully. Any engine or other problem during the flight would have forced Capt. Cunningham to jettison the external load immediately. Fortunately all went well during the short

The H-21, with crated forward hull slung below, flying between Foss Lake and Kapuskasing. (R. W. Bradford/NAM 16932)

flight and the HS-2L hull was deposited safe and sound at the airport. All concerned breathed a sigh of relief. That evening all attended a dinner to celebrate the successful operation. The next day, crew members prepared the recovered components for truck transport to the Museum at Rockcliffe, tidied up the campsite and arranged for canoes, oil drums and other remaining equipment to be flown out. Before leaving the camp for the last time McIntyre carved an inscription on a wooden plaque, which read: "Foss Lake, G-CAAC recovered, National Aeronautical Collection, NMST, September 1969."

On September 17 a large tractor trailer loaded with the components proceeded to the Museum. On arrival the recovered components were given additional treatment with fresh applications of the Carbowax solution by brush, spray or immersion. Special shelving and containers were fabricated to store the smaller items safely. *La Vigilance* was now ready for a new career as a particularly significant exhibit of Canada's aeronautical heritage.

Chapter 8

THE RESTORATION

Though most assumed it was called Foss Lake, the small lake that G-CAAC had crashed in had no official name. So Bob Bradford applied to the Canadian Permanent Committee on Geographical Names, Department of Energy Mines and Resources, to have the lake named "Foss Lake." Shortly after the components arrived at Rockcliffe the Committee sent word of their approval.

The next question to be addressed was the immediate future of the recovered hull and components. There was some enthusiasm, particularly among friends and supporters outside the Museum, for an immediate start of the restoration of recovered items. However, careful consideration quickly resulted in a decision to maintain the historical integrity of the artifact by preserving and displaying it in the "as recovered" condition. At the same time, planning for a reproduction of G-CAAC using as many original HS-2L parts as possible was in the works. This proved to be a sensible and proper course of action and, in fact, formed the basis for the Museum's conservation/restoration policy, which has been followed ever since. Work commenced on a display base for the hull and was completed in June 1970. The hull, with a selection of other interesting components, tools, and equipment was placed on display. It proved to be a popular attraction for a number of years. Among the many visitors who made special trips to see *La Vigilance* at Rockcliffe, Stuart Graham, Madge Graham and Don Foss were particularly welcome as they came to renew their acquaintances with an aircraft they certainly never expected to see again. One poignant moment that remains fondly in memory is Madge Graham whispering softly "good old bus, good old bus," as she stroked the hull gently during a visit in 1970.

Priorities and workload at the Museum made an early start on an HS-2L reproduction impossible. However, plotting, planning and acquisition of information and additional authentic HS-2L components for the project continued at a slow but steady pace for the next few years. A great stroke of good fortune had occurred even before the recovery when Bob Bradford had contacted Capt. L.C. Powell, USN, via the National Air and Space Museum of the Smithsonian Institution. Capt. Powell arranged the donation of a large quantity of Curtiss HS-2L blueprints. These represented about 60 per cent of a complete set and, combined with a copy of the original construction manual, proved invaluable during construction and restoration. Sorting and studying these drawings and documents proved useful in assessing and identifying the recovered components. At the same time, they gave a good indication of the extent of the daunting task

Madge Graham visiting "the good old bus" in 1970. (A.J. Shortt/NAM 15430)

that faced the Museum's small staff. The construction and restoration of a flying boat with a 23-m (74-ft) wingspan was a much larger task than anything the Museum had undertaken up to that time. Many friends and enthusiasts recommended that the project, or at least the construction of the hull, be subcontracted to professional boat-builders. However, the Museum staff felt too close to *La Vigilance* to turn the work over to strangers. It would be six years before starting the project, then another 12 years dogged with innumerable interruptions, technical problems and administrative hurdles before completing it. Yet the determination to succeed never wavered. Careful assessment of the recovered components confirmed that only a few items, mainly hardware and fittings, could be incorporated into the reconstruction. With this reality established, a search commenced for original components to make the reconstruction authentic.

In 1965 during a trip to California, Ken Molson, then Curator of the National Aviation Museum (NAM), learned from Frank Tallman that the Los Angeles County Museum (LACM) held an HS-2L. On contacting the Museum Molson learned that the hull had been scrapped due to deterioration from being stored outdoors. The wings, however, had survived despite being stored in an inaccessible

Pacific Marine Airways' NC652 Sunkist Kid during the 1920s. (Western Airlines/NAM 16914)

area. No attempts were made at this time to acquire the wings because of their difficult location and the obvious fact that much more would be required to begin an HS-2L project. During a 1969 trip to Los Angeles, Dr D.M. Baird managed to see the wings in one of the Museum's warehouses and learned that ownership was claimed by a private individual. In the summer of 1970 Fred Shortt of the NAC made a detailed assessment of the stored components at the LACM warehouse. He found that not only the wings had survived, but also all interplane struts, rigging wires, turnbuckles, horizontal and vertical tail surfaces, wing- and tail-support booms and many other associated components. The remains of U.S. registration NC652 could be discerned on the tattered wing fabric. This aircraft, named *Sunkist Kid,* had been operated by Pacific Marine Airways between Catalina Island and the California coast during the 1920s. At the same time James Zordich of the LACM confirmed that the HS-2L components were the property of Mr. Harry Provolt, a vintage aircraft enthusiast and builder. Shortt contacted him in Los Angeles immediately and worked out a tentative deal to exchange a World War I rotary engine and cash for the HS-2L components.

A formal agreement was later finalized and during the winter of 1970 an operational Clerget rotary engine was assembled from a partial engine and spare parts that had been stored at Rockcliffe. In February 1971 Harry Tate and Fred Shortt went to the LACM and literally "dug" the HS-2L components out of the warehouse from under all forms of hospital equipment from bedpans to X-ray machines, trucks, and cars from the Museum collection and sundry other heavy, awkward items. They tidied up the wings, tail surfaces and other items, prepared them for transport and left them to be

Centre section of NC652's upper wing as acquired from LACM with wire cables attached and some tattered fabric still in place. Its condition is typical of all the Sunkist Kid *components received. (A.J. Shortt/NAM 13926)*

picked up later. A Canadian Armed Forces Hercules transport flew the components to Ottawa in July 1971.

In October 1973 Bob Bradford and Fred Shortt acquired a few more original HS-2L items from the old OPAS hangar in Sault Ste. Marie. With permission from the Ontario Department of Lands and Forests, they spent a day digging through the hangar's loft, affection-

November 1975: construction of the new hull is underway. The steamed and formed ash keel member is held in place by the plywood jig. The first hull floor beams are also in place. The Museum's Fokker D VII is in the background. (K.M. Molson /NAM 10836)

ately called "Nellie's Room." A large number of HS-2L turnbuckles, rolls of rigging cable and an HS-2L control-column wheel were a few of the treasures they brought back to Rockcliffe. By this time a list of materials required for the HS-2L reconstruction and a test run at producing hull floor beams had resulted from sorting and studying the

HS-2L drawings, construction manual, and original components. Though a serious start on the project was still two years off, purchases of a wide variety of wood and other expensive, difficult-to-obtain materials were worked into the Museum's small operations budget. Gradually, as suitable materials were located and funds were allocated, an impressive stock of sitka spruce, pine, cedar, mahogany, ash, and oak was built up. Copper and brass nails, brass screws of various sizes, bolts of cotton, sheets of steel and copper, and many other items were also gathered. Staff slowly assembled a woodwork shop as funds were acquired to purchase a planer, joiner, sandblast cabinet, table saw, etc. These were all basic tools to the HS-2L project as well as to other restorations underway. An increase in staff at the Museum also helped to supplement the small group that had recovered G-CAAC. Ed Patten replaced Harry Tate, who sadly had died soon after the NC652 components for the project were acquired. Peter Jessen and Joe Dorn, both skilled cabinetmakers, joined the staff in 1972 and 1975 respectively. From 1970 to 1974 NAC staff members gained valuable experience with Curtiss flying boat construction methods by participating in a major NAC project, the restoration of the Museum's Curtiss Seagull. The unveiling of this impressive restoration project in March 1974 did much to convince many sceptics of the viability of the HS-2L project.

May 1976: ash hull frames steamed, formed, and installed. Bulkheads also installed. (K.M. Molson/ NAM 10795)

By mid-1975 the necessary materials and equipment had been obtained. In September a jig for the hull was fabricated and the ash keel strip, which was steamed and formed in a home-made steam tank, was installed in the jig. At long last, the reconstruction of G-CAAC was underway.

Work proceeded steadily over the next few years and the Museum crew optimistically estimated that they would complete the project in about six years. In fact, the metamorphosis of G-CAAC required over twice that time. The crew did not encounter significant problems with the construction or restoration, but work was constantly interrupted by a wide variety of other projects and problems. The maintenance and overhaul of both flying and display aircraft, the restoration of other aircraft such as the Messerschmitt Me163B, the acquisition of new aircraft, and the production of other

October 1976: installation of mahogany stringers stabilize the hull frames and hint at the impressive shape of the hull. (K.M. Molson/NAM 11650)

November 1976: the upper hull's 5/₁₆-in. pine planking begins. The planking is secured to the ash frames with brass screws and to the mahogany stringers with brass nails. The nails are clinched over from the inside. (K.M. Molson/NAM 11654)

September 1977: Peter Jessen (left) and Joe Dorn complete installation of the sponsons. (A.J. Shortt/ NAM 12269)

September 1977: Peter Jessen and René Chevalier roll the hull to an inverted position. (J. Dorn /NAM 16110)

November 1977: Joe Dorn installs the first layer of $^5/_{32}$-in. mahogany planking at 45° on the hull's bottom. (A.J. Shortt /NAM 12245)

displays were only a few of the projects that took precedence over the HS-2L project. Despite these interruptions, work continued to move along.

Construction of the hull was difficult and very time-consuming due to the large number of wood bulkheads, frames and stringers,

Joe Dorn shapes and fits the coaming for the forward gunner/photographer position, typical of the many complex wood components manufactured for the project. (A.J. Shortt/NAM 14010 and 15094)

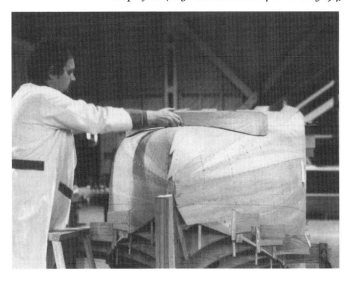

June 1981: Bill Merrikin and Barry Mackeracher take advantage of good weather to glue the fabric covering over the upper-hull planking. (A.J. Shortt/NAM 14783)

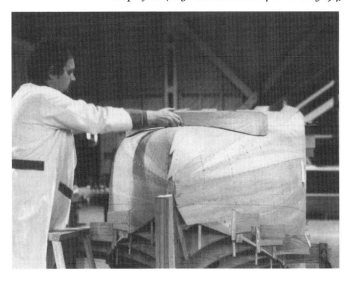

Peter Jessen installs mahogany stringers on the upper surface of the starboard sponson. (A.J. Shortt/NAM 12271)

May 1979: the hull is structurally complete. All cockpit, passenger and photographer positions are finished and a trial installation of the empennage has been made. The Museum's Hispano HA-1112 is in the background. (A.J. Shortt/NAM 13762)

metal fittings, and other components that had to be manufactured. Planking the compound curves of the hull severely tested the crew's skill and patience, but the results, as shown in the photographs, were spectacular. The upper hull was planked with $5/16$-in. pine over ash frames and mahogany stringers (battens in Curtiss terminology). The sponsons, or fins as they were called by Curtiss, were then built onto the sides of the forward hull. Two large circular plywood forms were constructed, fitted to the hull, and used to roll the hull inverted. The hull bottom was planked with two layers of $5/32$-in. mahogany.

The first layer was installed at 45° to the keel, then after a layer of fabric was glued on, a second layer of mahogany planking was installed parallel to the keel. The hull was then rolled upright again and the sponson planking was completed. Upper and lower planking were

G-CAAC's camera-port framing and plug are preserved and restored for installation in the new hull. (A.J. Shortt/NAM 13213)

Hull bow shows the completed camera and camera-sight ports. (A.J. Shortt/NAM 13216)

Starboard lower main-wing panel from NC652. Its condition is typical of all wing and empennage panels prior to restoration. (J. Dorn/NAM 15539)

Joe Dorn disassembles one of the wing-extension panels, a tedious and exacting task required for each panel. The Museum's Consolidated Canso is in the background. (A.J. Shortt/NAM 13489)

Ribs from a wing-extension panel, repaired, preserved, and ready for reassembly. If a large or small component is replaced or repaired with new wood or metal, the new item is identified with a permanent NAM stamp. (J. Dorn/NAM 14334)

Joe Dorn restores one of NC652's elevators. Complete disassembly, preservation, repair and in some cases replacement of some components is typical of the work that each wing and empennage panel requires. (A.J. Shortt/NAM 13363)

fastened to stringers with literally thousands of brass nails and to frames and floor beams with thousands of brass screws. This long, arduous process caused considerable ribald comments from those not involved in the process. After all planking was completed, openings for the bow gunner/photographer position and passenger locations were cut, then complex coamings were manufactured and

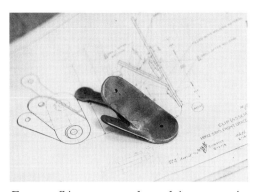

Even small items are complex and time-consuming to manufacture. This clip for one of the horizontal stabilizer brace wires is typical of a large number of such items manufactured by NAM for the project. (A.J. Shortt/NAM 17979)

installed in the openings. The final step in completion of the hull was a layer of fabric glued to the planking, completely covering the beautiful woodwork.

Far less visually impressive to visitors, and less rewarding in the form of their appreciative comments, was the difficult, tedious, and massive job of restoring the wings, empennage and other components from NC652. These components were naturally prized as original HS-2L items, which would make the finished aircraft a reconstruction rather than a replica. But it was noted many times, usually in jest, that it would have been simpler to construct new wings and tail feathers. The extent of this massive task is difficult to imagine but can at least be put in perspective: the HS-2L has eleven

Peter Jessen and Joe Dorn in the workshop hangar with the four main wing panels. The complete group also included 19 smaller panels plus struts, floats, cables, etc. (A.J. Shortt/NAM 15008)

separate wing panels (each one braced internally by wire cables), four ailerons, six tail-surface panels, two anti-skid panels, two wing floats, sixteen interplane struts, four lower centre-section struts, four horizontal stabilizer support struts, and two large complex booms that brace the wing and tail. All of these items are secured and supported externally by more than 60 individual wire cables, each manufactured to a precise length with a turnbuckle component spliced on each end. The wings had an interesting variety of rib configurations and minor structural variations, probably indicating manufacture by two or more contractors.

The completed HS-2L instrument panel with restored original instruments. (K.M. Molson /NAM 17269)

Ed Patten proudly displays the completed Liberty 12 engine. (A.J. Shortt /NAM 13723)

There is not much glamour involved in restoration work. Using chemicals and elbow grease Ed Patten works on the Liberty crankcase. (A.J. Shortt /NAM 13066)

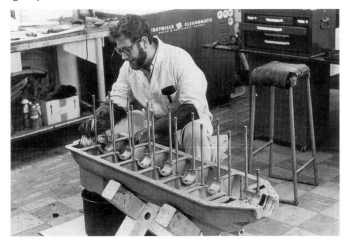

Some components of the disassembled Liberty engine ready for preservation. (A.J. Shortt /NAM 14131)

In addition to the spectacular hull and the less exciting but massive profusion of wing and tail panels, there was an enormous quantity of large and small items to be restored or manufactured. Complex metal fittings and other components, such as fuel tanks and fuel gauges, control column and rudder bars, instruments and instrument panel, camera and camera-sight ports and plugs, were produced in a seemingly endless stream. Many techniques and skills were recalled or developed, including sheet-metal work, welding, wire-cable splicing, chemical treating and electroplating. With both skill and ingenuity, Bill Merrikin, Chuck Aylen and Barry Mackeracher produced many beautiful items for the project and spent long hours with some of the more tedious tasks, such as cadmium plating

Barry Mackeracher and Bill Merrikin manufacture a new fuel tank. No remains of the original G-CAAC tanks were recovered. Legend has it that they were recovered soon after the crash and used for moonshine production. (A.J. Shortt/NAM 15013)

Chuck Aylen restores the radiator recovered from the crash site of G-CAOS. (J. Dorn/NAM 14520)

Completed fuel tanks installed aft of the cockpit. The restored G-CAAC fuel-flow sight gauge is mounted on the bulkhead fairing between the cockpit and the fuel-tank bay. Control cables and pulleys are visible at the rear of the bay. (A.J. Shortt/NAM 17838)

Functional fuel-contents gauges and mechanisms manufactured by NAM staff. (A.J. Shortt /NAM 15011)

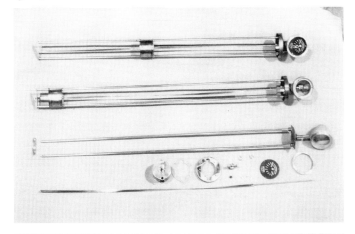

Chuck Aylen works on the restoration of the horizontal stabilizer. (A.J. Shortt/ NAM 13126)

A completed horizontal stabilizer, ready for fabric covering, hangs safely on the workshop wall. (K.M. Molson /NAM 15836)

The old and the new: some new fuel-pump components with original parts that were used for reference. (A.J. Shortt /NAM 16117)

NAM manufactured functional wind-driven, fuel-pump, and fuel-system components. (A.J. Shortt/ NAM 15033)

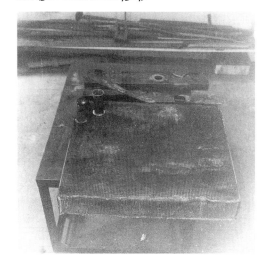

The radiator as recovered from the G-CAOS crash site. (J. Dorn/NAM 14314)

endless quantities of fittings and turnbuckles or manufacturing literally miles of rigging and control cables. With skill and patience Ed Patten spent many hours restoring an original Packard-built 360 hp Liberty 12 engine, manufacturing some missing items and "borrowing" from other Liberty engines in the collection. A valve-spring compressor, one of the tools recovered from the silt of Foss Lake, proved functional and very useful during the restoration. As public interest in the project grew, many individuals came forward with generous donations of HS-2L components that were invaluable to the project. Control wheels, propeller blades, fittings, turnbuckles, and other items were greatfully received and incorporated.

OPAS G-CAOS Snipe. (C.A. Schiller/NAM 18171)

The Western Canada Aviation Museum (WCAM) had located another HS-2L crash site on the Kenogami River near Longlac, Ontario. It was the remains of an OPAS HS-2L, G-CAOS (ex-USN A1250), named *Snipe*, which had made a forced landing due to engine failure October 7, 1927. Pilot R.E. Nicol and crew members J. Tyrell and D. Reid had all survived and the only serious injury was a broken leg sustained by Reid. As for *Snipe*, it was a write-off and had to be abandoned. Nicol, retired in the U.K., provided an interesting account of the event and technical details about the HS-2L that were valuable to the project, particularly those on the complex fuel management system.

In August 1976 Bill Merrikin, Joe Dorn and Peter Jessen from NAC, Murray Clearwater of WCAM and volunteer divers P. Massicotte of Longlac, Constables D. Ray, D. Longworth, and J. Osborn of the Ontario Provincial Police spent several days at the crash site. Without the protective benefits of a silt-covered lake bottom the aircraft did not survive in the manner that G-CAAC did, but the team did

Wing and empennage panels, with fabric covering stitched on, stand ready beside the hull for a turn in the paint shop. (K.M. Molson/NAM 17901)

Barry Mackeracher, Charlie Colwell, and Steve Payne juggle the port upper main-wing panel into position. Assembling an aircraft of this size with minimal equipment requires considerable ingenuity and dexterity. (A.J. Shortt/NAM 16442)

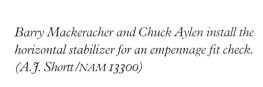

Barry Mackeracher and Chuck Aylen install the horizontal stabilizer for an empennage fit check. (A.J. Shortt/NAM 13300)

recover the Liberty engine, the radiator and a large quantity of castings and metal fittings. WCAM eventually displayed the engine while the castings, fittings and radiator proved invaluable to the G-CAAC project.

As the project entered the 1980s a great deal of the work had been accomplished. The hull was substantially completed and work progressed steadily on interior and cockpit details, camera ports, fuel tanks and fuel system, control cables, crew and passenger seats, and many other unseen but vitally important, installations and details. The wings and other flying surfaces were completed regularly and hung on a wall of the old workshop hangar out of harm's way.

In 1982 a traumatic series of events began when the Minister of Communications, the Honourable Francis Fox, convinced Cabinet to allot funds for construction of a new National Aviation Museum. From that moment on it became imperative to complete the HS-2L in time for the opening of the new building. Many other projects were suddenly required for the same reason. The small staff was gradually augmented and reorganization of the Museum combined the Aviation and Space Division and the National Aeronautical Collection and brought all staff together at Rockcliffe as the National Aviation Museum (NAM).

With hull, wing, and tail surfaces complete, the crew carried out a series of trial assemblies. Resembling high-wire artists, they worked high above the hangar floor on scaffolding and platforms, installing

Peter Jessen and Joe Dorn position the hull while George Kearney and Barry Mackeracher guide the engine onto its mount for the first installation check. Dorothy Fields, NAM administrative officer, looks on with concern. (A.J. Shortt/NAM 15687)

Engine installation with radiator and wing centre section in place. The radiator shutters were manufactured using a few badly corroded G-CAAC components and photographs for reference. (K.M. Molson/NAM 16870)

On November 22, 1984, the HS-2L, completely assembled but with no fabric on the wing or empennage panels, is moved from hangar 68 to the new NAM workshop. (J. Dorn/NAM 17235)

first the tail, then the engine mount, engine, and radiator. Finally they mounted the wings in place and for the first time the astounding size of the complete HS-2L could be appreciated. These trial assemblies established the correct fit of the various components and established correct rigging cable lengths.

The final trial assembly of the complete aircraft was accomplished in the fall of 1984 and at about the same time the Museum moved into a new workshop, which was established in a former STOL airline hangar about one kilometre across the airfield. On a cold and windy November 22, 1984, the completely assembled G-CAAC was carefully towed from the old hangar to the new workshop.

Now in its final stages, the project still required a great deal of difficult, finely detailed work. Acres of aircraft-grade cotton fabric had to be cut to size, sewn into sleeves and stitched to the wing and empennage panels. The panels then had to be sprayed with several coats of nitrate and buterate dope and finally with silver finishing coats. Engine and flying-control pulleys, cables and other components were completed and installed in the hull, wing and tail panels, ready for hookup on final assembly. A complex network of valves and copper tubing forming the fuel supply and management system was installed. The hull was finished with silver dope – a major task as the hull was almost as big as the paint shop it was sprayed in.

It was an emotional moment for the author when in the spring of 1986 he began the layout of the registration letters for the hull, wing, and tail markings. This emotion was shared by all the associated Museum staff as final tasks on G-CAAC were completed. It was clear now that the seemingly endless HS-2L project was reaching completion and as staff prepared to open the new Museum building a new era dawned for NAM.

During June 1986 as the final touches were applied, every staff member from either the administration office or the workshop was

Public unveiling ceremony of the HS-2L, May 13, 1988. (J. McQuarrie/NAM 21007)

Final assembly of the completed aircraft outside the NAM workshop, July 8, 1986. The anti-skid panels on the upper wings were too high to clear the hangar door. (A.J. Shortt/NAM 25149)

Barry Mackeracher notes the similarity between the fuel-control manifold that he has just completed and the bagpipes that he piped G-CAAC ashore with 14 years before. (J. Dorn/NAM 15566)

Completed cockpit with the U.S. Naval Air Corps serial number A1876 on the cockpit side. (K.M. Molson/NAM 18261)

NAM staff with the completed aircraft, July 8, 1986. Left to right: B.D. (Barry) Mackeracher; Philip Roger; Kelly Cameron; C.F. (Chuck) Aylen; William Merrikin; Joe Dorn; John Bradley; Charles Colwell; Lise Villeneuve; R.W. (Bob) Bradford; Steve Payne; E.C. (Ed) Patten; Claudette St-Hilaire; Keith Wilson; Geoffrey Cook; A.J. (Fred) Shortt; H.P. (Peter) Jessen. Absent: Dorothy Fields; George Kearney; Greg Dorning; Chris Peach. (A.J. Shortt/NAM 18262)

G-CAAC on display at NAM. The preserved original hull is displayed under the wing of the reconstruction. (J. Dorn/NAM 21684)

Complete at last, the reconstruction of G-CAAC ready to be photographed July 8, 1986. (K.M. Molson/NAM 18249)

involved in some way preparing the magnificent aircraft for its public debut. Final assembly took place in the first week of July and on July 8, 1986, G-CAAC was towed out of the workshop and into the sunshine to be photographed. Word of the photo session had spread and a large group of Museum staff, enthusiasts and other interested people were on hand to admire the finished aircraft. G-CAAC was at last ready for display and was moved into the new Museum building as work on the building structure was being completed. On May 13, 1988, a public unveiling ceremony was held in the new facility with U.S. Ambassador Thomas Niles and other dignitaries in attendance. On June 17, 1988, the new Museum opened and Canada's first commercial aircraft was at last on public view – a major star in a magnificent new showcase of aeronautical history.

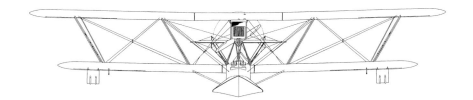

PART III

THREE-VIEW DRAWINGS

AND SPECIFICATIONS

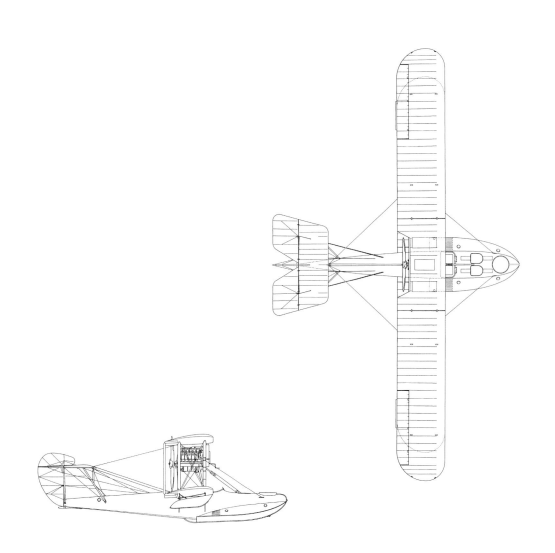

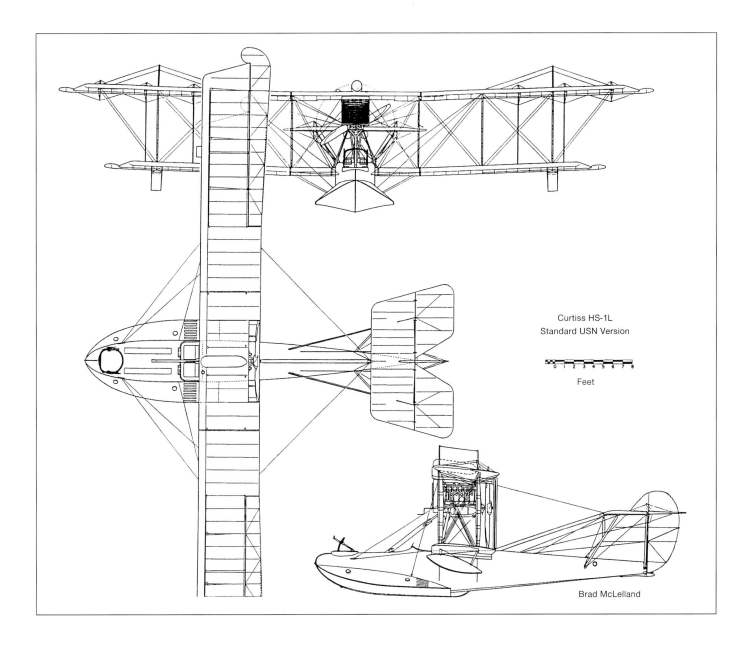

Curtiss HS-1L
Standard USN Version

0 1 2 3 4 5 6 7 8
Feet

Brad McLelland

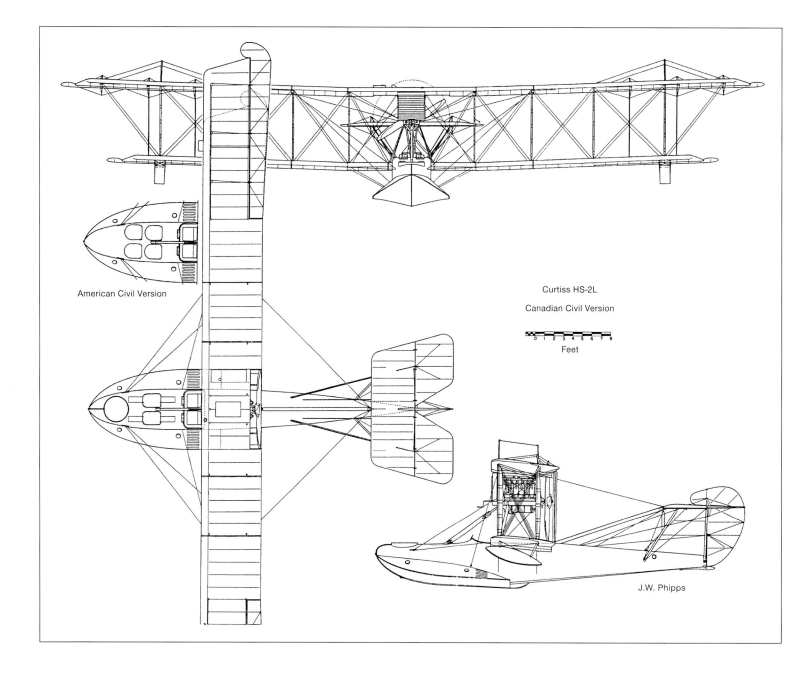

American Civil Version

Curtiss HS-2L

Canadian Civil Version

0 1 2 3 4 5 6 7 8
Feet

J.W. Phipps

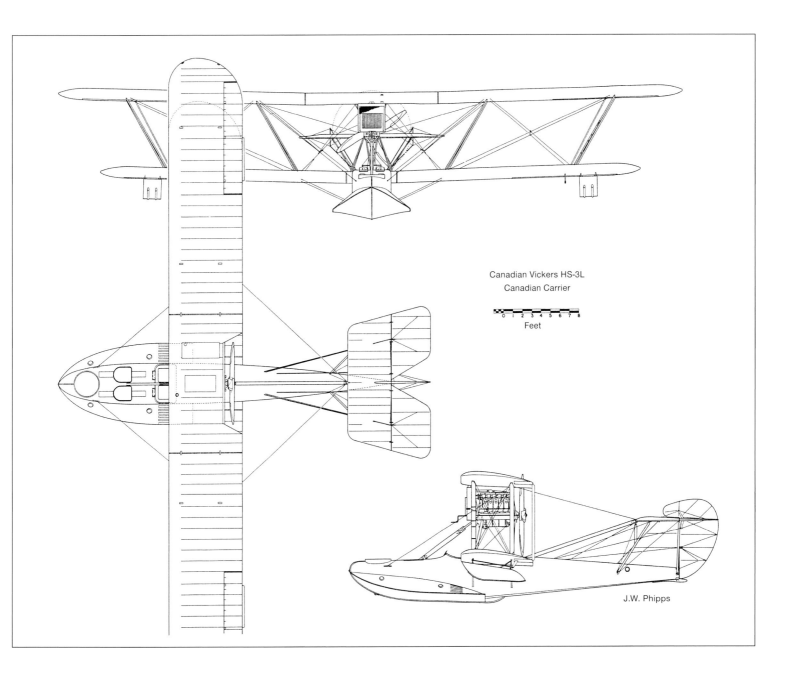

Canadian Vickers HS-3L
Canadian Carrier

Feet

J.W. Phipps

SPECIFICATIONS AND

PERFORMANCE

Model	Curtiss HS-1	Curtiss HS-1L
power plant	*200 hp Curtiss V2*	*360 hp Liberty*
Dimensions		
Wingspan, upper	59 ft 4 in. (18.08 m)	62 ft 5/16 in. (18.90 m)
Wingspan, lower	45 ft 8 in. (13.92 m)	52 ft 1 5/16 in. (15.88 m)
Chord, upper & lower	6 ft 3 5/32 in. (1.91 m)	6 ft 3 5/32 in. (1.91 m)
Incidence, upper	4 °	5 1/2 °
Incidence, lower	4 °	4 °
Dihedral, upper & lower	0 °	2 °
Stagger	0 °	0 °
Wing section	RAF NO. 6	RAF NO. 6
Gap at front spar	7 ft 6 in. (2.29 m)	7 ft 7 1/2 in. (2.32 m)
Gap at rear spar	n/a	7 ft 5 7/8 in. (2.28 m)
Length overall	38 ft 6 in. (11.74 m)	38 ft 5 15/16 in. (11.73 m)
Height	14 ft 3 in. (4.34 m)	14 ft 7 1/4 in. (4.45 m)
Areas		
Wing, incl. ailerons	626 sq. ft (58.15 m²)	653 sq. ft (60.66 m²)
Ailerons★	108 sq. ft (10.03 m²)	104.2 sq. ft (9.68 m²)
Horiz. stabilizer	63.9 sq. ft (5.94 m²)	54.8 sq. ft (5.09 m²)
Vert. stabilizer	34.9 sq. ft (3.24 m²)	19.6 sq. ft (1.82 m²)
Rudder	25 sq. ft (2.32 m²)	19.6 sq. ft (1.82 m²)
Elevators	49.8 sq. ft (4.63 m²)	45.6 sq. ft (4.24 m²)
Non-skid panels	n/a	16.9 sq. ft (1.57 m²)
Weights		
Empty, incl. water	3,215 lb (1 458.3 kg)	4,070 lb (1 846.1 kg)
Fuel & oil	670 lb (303.91 kg)	875 lb (396.9 kg)
Crew	320 lb (145.15 kg)	360 lb (163.3 kg)
Armament or load	–	510 lb (231.3 kg)
Gross	4,205 lb (1 907.39 kg)	5,910 lb (2 680.8 kg)
Performance		
Speed, maximum	73 mph (117.5 km/hr)	87 mph (140 km/hr)
Speed, landing	n/a	57 mph (91.7 km/hr)
Climb in 10 minutes	500 ft (152.4 m)	1,725 ft (525 m)
Max altitude attained	n/a	n/a
Endurance, max. speed	n/a	3.9 hrs
Endurance, cruise speed	n/a	5.0 hrs

★ These figures are not applicable to Boeing-built HS-2Ls with enlarged ailerons on upper wing and no ailerons on lower wing.

Curtiss HS-2L	*Curtiss HS-3L*	*Canadian Vickers HS-3L*
360 hp Liberty	*360 hp Liberty*	*360 hp Liberty*

74 ft $^5/_8$ in. (22.57 m)	75 ft 6 in. (23 m)	64 ft 6 in. (19.66 m)
64 ft 1 $^5/_8$ in. (19.55 m)	61 ft 5 in. (18.72 m)	55 ft 9 in. (16.99 m)
6 ft 3 $^1/_8$ in. (1.91 m)	6 ft 3 $^1/_8$ in. (1.91 m)	7 ft 6 in. (2.29 m)
5 $^1/_2$ °	5 $^1/_2$ °	3 °
4 °	4 °	1 $^1/_2$ °
2 °	2 °	1 $^1/_2$ °
0 °	0 °	2 $^1/_2$ °
RAF NO. 6	RAF NO. 6	Clark Y
7 ft 7 $^1/_2$ in. (2.32 m)	7 ft 7 $^1/_2$ in. (2.32 m)	7 ft 9 $^1/_4$ in. (2.37 m)
7 ft 5 $^7/_8$ in. (2.28 m)	7 ft 5 $^7/_8$ in. (2.28 m)	n/a
39 ft (11.89 m)	38 ft 7 in. (11.76 m)	39 ft (11.89 m)
14 ft 7 $^1/_4$ in. (4.45 m)	14 ft 7 $^1/_4$ in. (4.45 m)	13 ft 6 in. (4.11 m)
803 sq. ft (74.6 m²)	824 sq. ft (76.55 m²)	820 sq. ft (76.18 m²)
104.2 sq. ft (9.68 m²)	91 sq. ft (8.45 m²)	n/a
54.8 sq. ft (5.09 m²)	54.8 sq. ft (5.09 m²)	54.8 sq. ft (5.09 m²)
19.6 sq. ft (1.82 m²)	19.6 sq. ft (1.82 m²)	19.6 sq. ft (1.82 m²)
26 sq. ft (2.41 m²)	26 sq. ft (2.41 m²)	26 sq. ft (2.41 m²)
45.6 sq. ft (4.24 m²)	45.6 sq. ft (4.24 m²)	45.6 sq. ft (4.24 m²)
16.9 sq. ft (1.57 m²)	16.9 sq. ft (1.57 m²)	n/a
4,360 lb (1 977.7 kg)	4,550 lb (2 063 kg)	4,670 lb (2 118.31 kg)
977 lb (443.17 kg)	897 lb (406.88 kg)	930 lb (421.84 kg)
360 lb (163.3 kg)	360 lb (163.3 kg)	360 lb (163.3 kg)
625 lb (283.5 kg)	625 lb (283.5 kg)	548 lb (248.57 kg)
6,432 lb (2 917.55 kg)	6,432 lb (2 917.55 kg)	6,500 lb (2 948.4 kg)
85 mph (136.8 km/hr)	89 mph (143 km/hr)	87 mph (140 km/hr)
54 mph (86.9 km/hr)	54 mph (86.9 km/hr)	47 mph (75.6 km/hr)
1,800 ft (548.6 m)	n/a	360 ft/min (109.7 m/min)
10,900 ft (3 322.3 m)	n/a	6,000 ft (1 829 m)
4.4 hrs	5.3 hrs	n/a
6.3 hrs	n/a	n/a

CHRONOLOGY

Highlights in the Story of the HS Flying Boats

Late June 1917	Harold Kantner flies the HS-1 prototype at Buffalo, New York.
October 10, 1917	David McCulloch flies the HS-1 with the first 12-cylinder Liberty engine installed.
January 4, 1918	The Curtiss Aeroplane and Motor Co. ships A800, the HS-1L prototype, to the United States Navy (USN).
May 16, 1918	A1599, a modified H-1L and precursor to the HS-2L, is tested at Buffalo, New York, with a 1.83 m (6 ft) extension added to each wing.
May 24, 1918	The first eight HS-1Ls arrive at Pauillac, France, the first of which is flown on June 11.
July 15, 1918	Curtiss Aeroplane and Motor Co. ships A1820, the first HS-2L, to Miami Naval Air Station (NAS).
June 5, 1919	A1876 is the first HS-2L placed in civil service, operated by the St. Maurice Forest Protective Association at Dartmouth, Nova Scotia.
January 1920	Aero Ltd. uses HS-2Ls to start the first regular air service in North America since World War I, flying between Miami and Nassau and Bimini, British West Indies. Aero Ltd commissions the first civil HS-2L conversion.
June 4, 1922	Pacific Marine Airways starts a scheduled air service between Los Angeles and Catalina Island with HS-2Ls. The route is taken over by Western Air Express in 1928, continuing to use HS-2Ls until 1929. Though service is temporarily interrupted in 1923, it is the longest operating air service in North America of its time.
May 23, 1924	Laurentide Air Service starts the first scheduled air service in Canada between Angliers, Quebec and the Quebec Goldfields using HS-2Ls.
October 1, 1928	The USN strikes A1185, its last HS-2L, from its records at Hampton Roads NAS.

November 1, 1932	G-CAOA, G-CAOK, and G-CAOQ, the last three Curtiss HS-2Ls to fly anywhere, return to their Ontario Provincial Air Service (OPAS) base on or about this date. G-CAOA logged 2 251 flying hours in its nine years of service with the OPAS, more hours in flight than any other HS-2L.
September to October 1968	The National Aviation Museum (NAM) salvages parts of HS-2L A1876/G-CAAC, Canada's first bush plane, from Foss Lake in Ontario. During August and September 1969, NAM salvages the remaining parts and a large portion of the hull.
July 1971	NAM obtains the wings and tail surfaces of Pacific Marine Airways HS-2L 652.
September 1975	NAM starts construction of a new HS-2L hull from drawings supplied by the USN.
August 1976	NAM and the Western Canada Aviation Museum salvage parts of OPAS HS-2L G-CAOS/A1250 from the Kenogami River near Longlac, Ontario.
June 1986	NAM completes the reconstruction of G-CAAC. It is the sole surviving HS flying boat anywhere.
June 17, 1988	G-CAAC goes on public display with the opening of NAM's new building at Rockcliffe Airport.

BIBLIOGRAPHY

Books

Aeronautical Chamber of Commerce. *The Aircraft Yearbook.* New York: Aeronautical Chamber of Commerce of America, 1919–1924.

Bowers, Peter M. *Curtiss Aircraft, 1907–1947.* London: Putnam, 1979.

Brock, Horace. *Flying the Oceans: A Pilot's Story of Pan Am 1935–1955.* Lunenburg, VT: Stinehour Press, 1978.

Bruno, Harry. *Wings Over America.* New York: Robert M. McBride, 1943.

Canon, Capt. Walter C. *The U.S. Coast Guard.* New York: Franklin Watts, 1965.

Davies, R.E.G. *Airlines of the United States Since 1914.* London: Putnam, 1972.

Dickey, Philip S. *The Liberty Engine, 1918–1942.* Washington, DC: Smithsonian Institution Press, 1968.

Elliott, Maj. John M. *The Official Monogram U.S. Navy and Marine Corps Aircraft Color Guide.* Vol. 1, 1911–1939. Boylston, MA: Monogram Aviation Publications, 1987.

Hassell, Col. Bert R.J. *Fish Hassell: A Viking with Wings.* Bend, OR: Maverick Publications, 1987.

Kennedy, Thomas Hart. *An Introduction to the Economics of Air Transportation.* New York: Macmillan, 1924.

Lee, Charles E., comp., and C.G. Grey, ed. *The Aircraft Yearbook.* London: Sampson, Low Marston, 1923.

Mersky, Peter B. *Marine Corps Aviation: 1912 to the Present.* Baltimore, MD: Nautical & Aviation Publishing Co. of America, 1987.

Molson, K.M. *Canada's National Aviation Museum: Its History and Collections.* Ottawa: National Aviation Museum, 1988.

——. *Pioneering in Canadian Air Transport.* Winnipeg, James A. Richardson & Sons, 1974.

Netto, Francisco C. Periera. *Avianco Militar Brasileira, 1916–1984.* Rio de Janeiro, n.d.

Pearcy, Arthur. *A History of U.S. Coast Guard Aviation.* Annapolis, MD: Naval Institute Press, 1989.

Rowe, Capt. Basil L. *Under My Wings.* Indianapolis: Bobbs-Merrill, 1956.

Santos, Enrique B. *Trails in Philippine Skies: A History of Aviation in the Philippines from 1909 to 1941.* Manila: Philippine Airlines, 1981.

Stevens, Robert W. *Alaskan Aviation History.* Vol. 2, 1929–1930. Des Moines, WA: Polynyas Press, 1990.

Swanborough, Gordon, and Peter M. Bowers. *United States Navy Aircraft Since 1911.* London: Putnam, 1968.

Trimble, William F. *Wings for the Navy: A History of the Naval Aircraft Factory, 1917–1956.* Annapolis, MD: Naval Institute Press, 1990.

United States. Navy Department. *The HS-1L Flying Boat Handbook.* Washington, DC, 1918.

——. Office of the Chief of Naval Operations. *United States Naval Aviation, 1910–1960.* Washington, DC, 1960.

Articles, Reports, Letters

Abbott, Dan-San. "Chinese Connection" [letter]. *Air Enthusiast* 38 (1989): 79.

———. "Rosamonde." *WWI Aero* 140 (May 1993): 17–26.

Bartlett, James A. "Those HS-2Ls!" *C.A.H.S. Journal* 20 (Fall 1982): 68–71, 82.

Bradford, R.W. "The Last Flight of *La Vigilance*." *C.A.H.S. Journal* 6 (1968): 93–98, 108.

———. "The Recovery of *La Vigilance*." *C.A.H.S. Journal* 8 (1970): 110–118.

Chung, Maj. De Senn. "Aviation in China." *Aviation and Aircraft Journal* 11 (October 31, 1921): 511–512.

Clarke, R. Wallace. "The Davis Gun." *Flypast* 40 (November 1984): 26–28.

Crone, Ray. "The Unknown Air Force." *C.A.H.S. Journal* 18 (Summer 1980): 41–48.

Leary Jr., Wm. M. "At the Dawn of Commercial Aviation: Inglis M. Uppercu and Aeromarine Airways." *Business History Review* 53 (Summer 1979): 180–193.

LeShane Jr., Albert A. "Aeromarine Airways, Inc." *American Aviation Historical Society Journal* 24 (Fall 1980): 162–180.

Matthews, Lt. Charles F. "History of U.S. Naval Aviation During the World War: Patrolling and Patrol Stations on the Western Atlantic." (unpublished) Washington, DC: U.S. Navy Department. Historical Section, n.d.

———. "U.S. Naval Air Stations in Canada: 1918." *C.A.H.S. Journal* 27 (Winter 1989): 135–142.

Maxwell, W.R. "Flying Boat Operations in Northern Ontario: 1920." *C.A.H.S. Journal* 11 (Fall 1973): 89–94.

Molson, K.M. "The Canadian Search for Nungesser & Coli." *C.A.H.S. Journal* 15 (Summer 1977): 62.

———. "Laurentide Air Service: A History of Canada's First Scheduled Air Service." *C.A.H.S. Journal* 21 (Fall 1983): 68–85.

Redden, Charles F. "Over Water Flying for 1923." *U.S. Air Services* (January 1923): 25–27.

Richardson, H.C. "Aeroplane and Seaplane Engineering." *Aerial Age Weekly* 9 (February 24, 1919): n.p.

Shortt, A.J. "Museum Update." *C.A.H.S. Journal* 19 (1981): 77–81.

Tully, T.B. "A Comparison Between the Curtiss HS-2L and Canadian Vickers Vedette Flying Boats and Other Aircraft." (unpublished) n.d.

Warner, Edward. "American Aircraft in China." *Aviation* 8 (1 February 1920): 19.

———. "The Paradox Plane." *Aviation* 26 (June 29, 1929): 2261.

———. "Type of Aircraft Used in Naval Aviation 1917–1919." *Navy Department Bulletin* 101 (December 1919).

Periodicals

The following periodicals were consulted extensively in the compilation of Part I: *Aerial Age Weekly, Aviation, Flying, U.S. Air Services.*

LIST OF ACRONYMS

AEA	Aerial Experiment Association
CAB	Canadian Air Board
CAHA	Connecticut Aeronautical History Association
CF	Canadian Forces
FAP	Força Aérea Portuguesa
GHCM	Glenn H. Curtiss Museum
LACM	Los Angeles County Museum
LWF	Lowe, Willard & Fowler Eng. Co.
NAC	National Aeronautical Collection
NAF	Naval Aircraft Factory
NAM	National Aviation Museum
NAS	Naval Air Station
NASM	National Air and Space Museum
NEAM	New England Air Museum
NMST	National Museum of Science and Technology
OBH	Ontario Bushplane Heritage
OPAS	Ontario Provincial Air Service
PAS	Philippine Air Service
RAF	Royal Air Force
RBCM	Royal British Columbia Museum
RCAF	Royal Canadian Air Force
RNAS	Royal Naval Air Service
ST. MFPA	St. Maurice Forest Protective Association Ltd.
SCAS	South China Air Service
SDAM	San Diego Aerospace Museum
SGDM	Servitos Gerais de Directas da Marinha
USAAS	United States Army Air Service
USAFM	United States Air Force Museum
USAS	United States Air Service
USCG	United States Coast Guard
USMC	United States Marine Corps
USN	United States Navy
USNA	United States National Archives
WAE	Western Air Express Inc.
WCAM	Western Canada Aviation Museum

INDEX